9

HOW TO BE SU

MW01031118

Accountability, Scripturally spe[...]
positive and negative will be rec[...] on God's computer system. This does
not mean that we will be responsible only for what we did. It also means
that we will be held responsible for what we did not do . . . and should have
done! You might call it a type of double entry bookkeeping.   Chapter 1

* * *

We limit the power of God. God does not want our sacrifice. God wants
OBEDIENCE!   Chapter 2

* * *

If our Father knows in advance what we have need of, why then do we pray?
                                                                     Chapter 4

* * *

Many people seek Christ not as Saviour, but as Santa Claus! They seek to
gain acceptance, popularity, financial success or physical healing. Their
motives are wrong.   Chapter 6

* * *

How sad that Americans have more time-saving devices and less time than
any other people in the world. They plan for their future on earth as though
time will stand still . . . yet they drive as though time is swiftly running out!
                                                                     Chapter 7

* * *

Christ does not judge our use of our talents by a worldly scale of popularity.
This is not a Miss America contest!   Chapter 8

* * *

It is better to have your bank in Heaven than to have heaven in a bank. The
day will soon come when you will become accountable for your treasures at
the Judgment Seat of Christ.   Chapter 9

* * *

To know God's will is man's greatest treasure. To do His will is life's greatest
privilege.   Chapter 10

* * *

**All this and <u>much more</u> you will find in the chapters of this exciting and
revealing book that shows** *How To Be Sure Of Crowns In Heaven!*

HOW
TO BE SURE
OF CROWNS
IN HEAVEN
by
SALEM KIRBAN

Published by SALEM KIRBAN, Inc., Kent Road, Huntingdon Valley, Pennsylvania, 19006. Copyright © 1981 by Salem Kirban.
Printed in the United States of America. All rights reserved, including the right to reproduce this book or portions thereof in any form.
ISBN 0-912582-34-0
Library of Congress Catalog Card No. 80-82067

DEDICATION

To **Rev. C. Ross Whitby**

In the summer of 1979, my wife and I had the privilege of getting to know Ross and Ada Whitby. We were vacationing at Montrose Bible Conference in Montrose, Pennsylvania. (It was here I had accepted Christ as my Lord and Saviour as a child.)

Rev. Whitby was then Pastor of Bethany Church in Wescosville, Pennsylvania. Our friendship grew and he invited me to bring a series of messages on Bible prophecy in his church. I recall that summer that we sat under a shade tree on the lawn of Torrey Lodge at Montrose Bible Conference. We talked over our early years at Montrose. Rev. Whitby graduated from Wheaton College in 1945. In those war years he served on the staff of Montrose Bible Conference and managed the Tea Room.

We met Ross and Ada again in summer, 1980 at Montrose Bible Conference. This time, Ross set a date for my series of Prophecy meetings. The dates were November 3, 4 and 5. It was on Labor Day that Ross confided to us he had cancer.

Monday night, November 3rd . . . we stopped in the parsonage where Ross and Ada lived . . . just a stone's throw from the church. He was not able to attend the meetings but he insisted that his wife, Ada, attend each session.

On Wednesday night, November 5th, after visiting with Ross . . . we shook hands and assured him of our prayers. That evening in the service, I felt led of God to sing a new chorus I recently learned . . . *All Things Work Together For Good To Them That Love The Lord.* It was written by friends of mine, Lee and Cindy Condran. On the spur of the moment, I invited Ada to come to the platform and sing along with me.

That night, upon returning home, we received a phone call from Ada. Ross had gone home to be with the Lord while the church service was in progress. Sunday, November 16, 1980, the church was packed for a Celebration of the Coronation of Rev. C. Ross Whitby. **The people loved him because he put others *first* in his life.** Ross was unassuming and humble. He gave Christ the pre-eminence! And a Crown of Glory awaits him in Heaven (1 Peter 5:2-4)!

IN APPRECIATION

HOW TO BE SURE OF CROWNS IN HEAVEN could not have become a reality without the prayerful dedication of the Lord's money entrusted to God's people. The below have shared in the distribution of this book and we are extremely grateful. In some instances the names listed are memorial gifts.

CONTENTS

ACKNOWLEDGMENTS

To **Dr. Gary G. Cohen,** President of Clearwater Christian College, Clearwater, Florida, who carefully checked the final manuscript.

To **Doreen Frick,** who devoted many hours proofreading the text.

To **Eileen Kirban,** for her artistic calligraphy.

To **Estelle Bair Composition,** for excellent craftsmanship in setting the type.

To **Walter W. Slotilock,** Chapel Hill Litho, for negatives.

To **Koechel Designs,** for an excellent cover design.

To **Dickinson Brothers, Inc.,** for printing this book.

WHY I WROTE THIS BOOK

It has been my privilege to speak in over 300 churches on the subject of Bible prophecy. There have been small churches of 30 people and large churches of 3000 people.

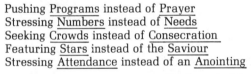

I sensed that those in the congregation were hungry for knowledge on what would happen next in God's timetable. Yet, I also felt that there was a void in the hearts of many who listened.

I wondered if we were too often measuring success by worldly standards. Many of us, in one way or another, were guilty of

> Pushing <u>Programs</u> instead of <u>Prayer</u>
> Stressing <u>Numbers</u> instead of <u>Needs</u>
> Seeking <u>Crowds</u> instead of <u>Consecration</u>
> Featuring <u>Stars</u> instead of the <u>Saviour</u>
> Stressing <u>Attendance</u> instead of an <u>Anointing</u>

Particularly in America, we seem to fly through life at breakneck speed. We began by traveling in ox-carts at four miles an hour, then horses at six miles an hour, then automobiles at 60 miles an hour and now airplanes at over 600 miles an hour. In this framework, we tend to lose the real values of life. Our goals and our priorities become warped.

Too often we measure success by material gains. God doesn't call us to be successful. He calls us to be faithful. And we whiz through life unconcerned about eternal values!

That's why I was burdened to write on a topic that most everyone would prefer not to hear . . . **ACCOUNTABILITY!** I began with the intention of simply writing a small booklet. But as I researched this subject, God opened up avenues that I had not originally considered. Thus, it became a full length book.

Romans 14:12 reminds us that *"every one of us shall give an account of himself to God!"* I am afraid in today's fast-paced life, we fail to grasp the real significance of this . . . eternally. Now is the time for you to seriously consider exactly <u>how you can be sure of Crowns in Heaven</u>. That's why I wrote this book!

Salem Kirban

Huntingdon Valley, Pennsylvania
U.S.A., January, 1981

1

THE MESSAGE NO ONE WANTS TO HEAR

Accountability, Scripturally speaking, is a time when <u>all</u> of our actions both positive and negative will be recalled on God's computer system.

* * *

This does not mean that we will be responsible only for what we did do. It also means that we will be held responsible for what we did <u>not</u> do ... and should have done! You might call it a type of double entry bookkeeping.

* * *

Every one will have to give an account of himself to God. For believers, there will be the Judgment Seat of Christ.

* * *

Do we know more about Gold than God? Are we more concerned daily about Silver than about Souls? Is our daily activity directed more to our House than our Heavenly Home? If so, we are building on a very weak, extremely worthless foundation!

* * *

God is not fooled by our actions. There will come a day when He will see through our plastic personality right into the very intents of our heart (1 Corinthians 4:5).

* * *

How odd that so many of us get so wrapped up in this 70 or so year time span of life and do no planning for eternal rewards?

1

THE MESSAGE NO ONE WANTS TO HEAR!

Unpopular Subject

This subject is a very unpopular one. Rarely is it preached in any church. For, if this message is delivered fully, it could swiftly deplete a congregation.

It is a message we would prefer not to hear. Why rock the boat! Let's believe what we want to believe. Let's keep our way of life uncluttered by the deep truths of God's Word. Let's instead skim over the surface of Scriptures. In that way, we will be in the majority. It will be easy to be a Christian and we won't have to give up anything!

The above is the thinking of most Christians. It would be safe to say that about 90% of believers today would not accept what is written in this book because it would mean they would have to change the lifestyle to which they have become comfortably accustomed.

Yet one day, and it may be soon, they will have to face the consequences!

Then, what is this subject that is rarely preached to its fullest?

ACCOUNTABILITY

We Will Be Held Responsible

Accountability is a big word but with a simple meaning. In essence, accountability means that we are and will be held responsible for our own acts.

Accountability, Scripturally speaking, is a time when all of our actions both positive and negative will be recalled on God's computer system. For the Christian . . . it will be a day of reckoning!

This does not mean that we will be responsible only for what we did do. It also means that we will be held responsible for what we did not do . . . and should have! You might call it a type of double entry bookkeeping.

Actually, the most frightening fact that we as Christians will have to face is this:

> . . . *every one of us*
> *shall give an account*
> *of himself*
> *to God!*
>
> (Romans 14:12)

Have you ever given much thought to this? You should!

Two Judgments

The Verse just quoted refers to a Universal Accountability. Every one will have to give an account of himself to God.

For believers, there will be the **JUDGMENT SEAT OF CHRIST.**

> This judgment will occur after the Rapture and during the Tribulation Period. The Judgment Seat of Christ will occur in Heaven. It is sometimes called *"the day of Christ."* See Philippians 1:10 and 2:16.

> This judgment differs from the **GREAT WHITE THRONE JUDGMENT** which is for unbelievers. Those sinners present at the Great White Throne Judgment are there because they have rejected God's salvation. Salvation is a present possession of the believer (Luke 7:50, John 3:36). Rewards, for the believer, are a future attainment, to be given after the Rapture (2 Timothy 4:8, Revelation 22:12).

> At the Judgment Seat of Christ, each believer will appear. Note

Sequence of Coming Judgments

carefully what will happen to you here:

> *For we must all appear*
> *before*
> *the judgment seat of Christ;*
> *that everyone may receive*
> *the things done in his body,*
> *according to* **what** *he hath done,*
> whether it be good or bad.
> (2 Corinthians 5:10)

Therefore judgment is based not only on what good we did while here on earth . . . but also that which we did which was bad! This judgment is not dealing with eternal penalties. Works are not a key to eternal life. After accepting Christ as Lord and Saviour of our life, works are, however, a key to our rewards.

It must be remembered that *". . . we are laborers together with God"* (1 Corinthians 3:9). We are, in effect, God's cultivated field. He looks to us, as a cultivated field, to bear fruit.

Cultivated Or Sub-standard

In our allotted life span of some 70 years, is our life a cultivated field that bears much fruit? Or does it reflect a sub-standard field that produces little crops! Are we more concerned about self and self-advancement and material possessions?

Do we know more about Gold than about God? Are we more concerned daily about Silver than about Souls? Is our daily activity directed more to our House than our

Heavenly Home? If so, we are building on a very weak, extremely worthless foundation.

This is why Christ reminds us:

> . . . *if any man*
> *build upon this foundation*
>   *gold, silver, precious stones,*
>   *wood, hay, stubble—*
> *Every man's work*
> *shall be made manifest*
>   *(shown for what it is)*
> *for the day shall declare it,*
> *because it shall be revealed*
>   *by fire;*
>   *and the fire*
>   *shall test*
>   *every man's work*
>   *of what sort it is.*
> *If any man's work abide*
>   *which he hath*
>   *built upon it,*
>   *he shall receive*
>   *a reward.*
> *If any man's work shall be burned,*
>   *he shall suffer*
>   *loss;*
>   *but he himself*
>   *shall be saved,*
>   *yet as*
>   *by fire.*
>
>   (1 Corinthians 3:12-15)

Rarely do we give thought to what the future holds for us in eternity. We do not seem to understand that it is what we do <u>here</u> in following our Saviour's guidelines that determines what our position will be eternally in Christ.

Our most prime daily considerations, for the most part, are related to selfish desires, selfish accomplishments and selfish goals. Isn't it a strange and rather sad reflection of believers that the best selling Christian books include those on how to lose weight. Food becomes our god and dieting the penalty!

Rewards Not Based On Popularity

Some of the best selling religious books are those that deal with money and those that relate the life of a famous living person who, perhaps had a *"spectacular"* salvation experience. He may be a motion picture star, a country and western singer, an important government figure or even a criminal. We tend to believe these people will have the greatest rewards in Heaven because of their popularity on earth.

Many Christian ministries, by placing these people in prominence, are guilty of perpetuating this myth either directly or indirectly.

But rewards are not based on man's evaluation. Rewards will be based on the Lord's estimate of their value. And the Lord knows the heart! See Acts 15:8. The widow who prayed faithfully each day for missionaries in Asia, or Africa may have far greater rewards. Our values here on earth have a tendency to be warped by popularity contests.

In All This Job Sinned Not!

Perhaps no one suffered more in so short a period of time as Job suffered. Satan was determined to undermine Job and used ungodly men and the elements of nature in his plan. Job's 7000 sheep, 3000 camels, 500 yoke of oxen and 500 donkeys were all stolen or burned up. Even his own family was killed!

To add to his misery, he had no comfort from his wife. She suggested: *"Curse God, and die"* (Job 2:9). How easy it would have been for Job to sin, to enjoy the pleasures of the world, to forsake God. What more could he lose? Everything was gone. Even his own wife did not support him with comfort and assurance. Yet, in spite of all these reverses, Job sinned not. What a lesson for us!

**Motives
Judged**

Not only will our works be examined, but also how well we have done these works and for what motives! The entire depth of our spiritual life, while on earth, will come up for review!

Our works will have no value if they are not built on Christ. Five different crown rewards will be given. Each person will receive rewards in relation to their individual service while on earth.

Rewards for service will be determined by our life here on earth.

> In measure as we shine here . . .
>   we shall shine in the day of His glory.
>   (Daniel 12:3)

> In measure as we labor here,
>   we shall have authority when He returns.
>   (Luke 19:17-19)

> In measure as we suffer here . . .
>   we shall have comfort for evermore.
>   (Matthew 5:10-12)

> In measure as we are soul-winners here...
>   we shall have joy and rejoicing in His presence.
>   (1 Thessalonians 2:19,20)

> In measure as we shepherd the flock here . . .
>   we shall be commended
>   when the Chief Shepherd appears.
>   (1 Peter 5:4)

Soul-winning, as an example is commendable. But soul-winning with the wrong motives will be judged of God. We are not engaged in a spiritual olympics to see how many souls our church can win to Christ.

When we become more concerned with numbers of souls won, we often resort to *"hot dog and baseball salvations."* There is nothing wrong with supplying youngsters with hot dogs and baseball activities. But when these activities are brought about by wrong motives . . . they become wrong. If the motive is one of numbers and bigness . . . it can lead to building a church of "surface Christians" with no spiritual depth.

It is far more responsible to personally and carefully cultivate a new Christian and nurture him into spiritual adulthood. God does not need us to win one soul to Christ! He does call us, however, to be witnesses. When we reach the point that we earnestly feel that one's salvation depends on our efforts . . . what we personally do . . . then our motives could be questioned by God.

No Magic Formula

There is no magic formula, as an example in giving an invitation. It is not necessary to sing a certain hymn . . . pose certain questions in a sequential order, or to count the uplifted hands. When such actions become our standard practice, our motives may need evaluating honestly in prayer before God.

God in His Word tells us:

> . . . *the Word of God . . .*
> *is a discerner*
>   *of the thoughts*
>   *and intents*
>   *of the heart.*
>
> (Hebrews 4:12)

God is not fooled by our actions. There will come a day when He will see through our plastic personality right into the very intents of our heart (1 Corinthians 4:5).

Our Life Today Prepares Us For Tomorrow

Every thought, every action is recorded by God and we will be held accountable. one might compare it to a final examination at school. Throughout the school term we are constantly learning. We know that what we are supposed to be learning will one day be put to a test. That test is called the final examination. If we have prepared for it and have been faithful, we enter the examination room full of confidence and strength.

On the other hand, if we made it a practice to do the least we could during that school term; if we missed classes, failed to apply ourself, that's different. We then enter the examination room with great fear and apprehension hoping against hope!

We do not have to wait until after the examination is over to know how we did. Our heart has already revealed to us our motives and we know already the approximate outcome.

The Tragedy of Disobedience

Lot made seven errors in choosing Sodom.

He **looked** toward Sodom (13:10).
He **leaned** toward Sodom (13:12).
He **lived** in Sodom (14:12).
He **legislated** for Sodom (19:1, 9).
He **lost** his testimony in Sodom (19:14).
He **learned** the ways of Sodom (19:32).
He **left behind** the fruit of his blacksliding with the emerging of both Moab and Ammon, who became enemies of God's people (19:37).

The people of Sodom, surrounded Lot's house attempting to impose their homosexuality on Lot's heavenly visitors. Lot, wishing to protect his visitors (in his thinking) selects the lesser of two evils and offers two daughters. Such an accommodation would turn the respected position of the woman over to the perverted lusts of the Sodomites.

The angels struck the Sodomites with blindness and directed Lot to leave the city. Lot's sons-in-law laughed in his face at what they took to be a joke . . . leave the city!

The tragedy of this disobedience is that only Lot, his wife and two daughters would leave. Six remained behind in Sodom.

Lot's wife probably looked back because she doubted her husband's Divine warning and witnessed the lush gardens, the city of orchards . . . everything that had been dear to her, vanish in fire and smoke. She failed life's *"examination test."*

The final day arrives. The marks are posted on the school bulletin board. And we either weep or rejoice!

The one difference between a school examination and a "life examination" is that there is no second chance! If we flunk out at school, we can take that course or courses over again and redeem ourself. But after we have spent our entire life and face the Judgment Seat of Christ, there is no re-exam! That's it!

**Rewards
Or
Emptiness**

God has handed us life on earth. He has allowed us, in eternal values, a short stay here. How well we follow through in His commands determines an accountability that results in crowns as rewards or emptiness!

How odd that we are often guilty of getting so wrapped up in this 70 or so year time span of life that we do no planning for eternal rewards!

What are some of the things we will be held accountable for?

✓ CHECKLIST FOR SPIRITUAL GROWTH

My Accountability

If "No" ... where do I stand spiritually, right now?

1. Does my daily life reflect greater priorities for God than for Gold (material possessions)?

   YES ☐   NO ☐   Totally Lacking ☐   Needs Improving ☐

2. Am I grateful enough for my salvation that I seek to witness to others about Christ?

   YES ☐   NO ☐   Totally Lacking ☐   Needs Improving ☐

3. Are my motives for soul winning purely based on that fact that Christ died for my sins?

   YES ☐   NO ☐   Totally Lacking ☐   Needs Improving ☐

   (If your motives for soul winning are to win a contest or simply to see numerical growth in your church ... then your basic motives are self-centered. You should check the "No" block.)

4. If Christ were to review your Christian life tomorrow, do you think you would come through with a "Well Done" mark?

   YES ☐   NO ☐   Totally Lacking ☐   Needs Improving ☐

If you have checked the TOTALLY LACKING Box ... it means that, in this specific category ... spiritually ... you are failing. You need to realign your priorities ... and strive for spiritual growth, now!

If you checked NEEDS IMPROVEMENT Box ... it means that you are striving for a fulfilled Christian life ... but recognize your need to make further improvements.

As a believer, God's measure of blessing and answered prayer in your life will be directly proportionate to your full obedience to His Word.

2

OUR ATTITUDE TOWARDS GOD

How often in our own life, we try to reason things out feeling we are doing God a favor. We seek to bend Scriptures to suit our particular circumstance. Then we make some type of sacrifice, like a donation to our church or a mission work, hoping that this will cover up our disobedience.

* * *

We limit the power of God. God does not want our sacrifice. God wants OBEDIENCE!

* * *

In your own life, it may not be riches which are standing between you and God. It may be possessions. It may be power. It may be prestige. Whatever it is, confess the sin and determine with God's help to follow Him. You will be held accountable!

* * *

Do you believe there can be prosperity in poverty? Of course! Can there be prosperity in trials? YES! Read James 1:2-4.

2

OUR ATTITUDE TOWARDS GOD

**It's The
Uplook
That
Counts!**

How do we think about God? How do we feel about God? Daily is our attitude one of <u>gratitude</u>? As a Christian does our daily walk reflect thankfulness that Christ died for our sins? Its not the outlook, but the uplook that counts!

I am reminded of the soldier, who, when facing the enemy . . . retreated. He was brought before Alexander the Great. Alexander, who fearlessly conquered the then-known world, looked down at this cowardly soldier and asked:

What is your name?

The soldier tearfully replied:

Sir, my name is Alexander.

Alexander the Great, stood up, pointed his finger at the soldier and in a loud voice boomed . . .

Sir . . .
either change your attitude
or change your name!

Does our life reflect ungratefulness, a complaining spirit, a self-centered motivation? Or does our life . . . daily . . . reflect an attitude of gratitude for God's unfailing, sacrificial love to us.

In what ways will we be held accountable for our attitude towards God?

A. In our <u>obedience</u> to God!

Saul was directed by God's appointed messenger, Samuel, to invade Amalek and destroy it completely . . . even the livestock. The Amalekites continually harassed Israel ever since their wilderness wanderings (Exodus 17:8–16).

Saul reasoned he had a better way and he saved King Agag and the best of the livestock supposedly for a sacrificial offering. When confronted by Samuel for this disobedience to God's directive, Saul attempted to place the blame on the people themselves. Samuel saw through this and told Saul:

> *To obey is better than sacrifice* . . .
> (1 Samuel 15:22)

Saul had placed <u>his own will</u> above <u>God's will</u>.

We Seek To Bend Scripture

How often in our own life, we try to reason things out feeling we are doing God a favor. We seek to bend Scriptures to suit our particular circumstance. Then we make some type of sacrifice, like a donation to our church or a mission work,

WHAT IS SEPARATION?

Paul admonishes Christians in 2 Corinthians 6:17 to *"... come out from among them, and be ye separate ..."*

First, in understanding this verse, we should use Christ as the model of separation.

He was:

1. **Separated from evil**
   His desires, His motives and acts were separated apart from this present world system which genders greed, selfishness, ambition and pleasure and seethes in national and commercial rivalries.

2. **Separated from conformity to the world**
   He came in contact with evil both in the world and in the church, but He did not become an accomplice or partner in this evil nor conform with it.

Separation in Scriptures includes **(a)** negatively, separation from whatever is contrary to the mind of God, and **(b)** positively, separation **unto** God Himself.

Although this is a humorous photograph ... it conveys the point. The children are in the barrel. The barrel is in the *"water"* but it is not part of the water.

Just as the barrel protects the children from being a part of the water ... so Christ is our Separator, encompassing us so that as faithful Christians we will be in the world, but **not a part of** its compromising influences.

WHAT IS SEPARATION?

You may recall that the Pharisees – whose very name, **Pharishim,** means *"separated ones"* – were separated but their separation was a mechanical, self-righteous separation. Their letter-strictness in following the oral laws of the fathers (extra-Biblical oral teachings) made them self-righteous and soon they would wash if they even so much as touched a Gentile.

Finally they became the foremost persecutors of Jesus Christ. They were extremely bitter when a woman, who was a sinner, washed Jesus' feet with her tears and wiped them with the hair of her head (Luke 7:36-39). They – unlike Jesus – were more interested in condemning this woman than seeing her saved.

We are **in** the world but we should be separate by not being **of** the world. Our separation **should be** from those who deny Christ as personal Saviour and Lord. We should not conform to their doctrines, their practices, their motives and their materialistic desires.

Note this: *Don't join* in a fellowship with unbelievers (verse 14);

> If in, **come out** (verse 17);
> If out, don't **touch** (verse 17)

Note also God's promise to those who will obey His call to *"come out"* –

> *"I will be a Father unto you . . ."* (verse 18).

This separation is **not** a separation from other Christians. To understand 2 Corinthians 6:17 in its context, read verses 14, 15 and 16 which relate to unbelievers, not to other Christians. Matthew 18:15-17 and 2 Thessalonians 3:14-15, however, do tell us the circumstances under which we should separate from other Christians. Do read both of these passages. Also see Romans 16:17.

hoping that this will cover up our disobedience.

Such disobedience is often seen in justifying separation and divorce among believers. It is often seen when a believer desires to marry an unbeliever. And sad to say, it is also explained away when Christian organizations who claim to be Bible believers unite in fellowship with other religious organizations who deny the foundations of Scripture and separation. These groups, in a desire for growth and popularity, sacrifice principles for power. This is sin! They try to cover up their misdeeds by saying that Christians should exercise love. But God's Word tells us:

> What agreement hath the temple of God
> with idols . . .
> Wherefore,
>   come out from among them,
>   and be ye separate . . .
> (2 Corinthians 6:16, 17)

We often reply that, *"Well, I understand that . . . but look how many souls are being won to Christ. They would have never been reached otherwise."*

God Wants Obedience

How foolish such a reply! **We limit the power of God!** This, on top of disobeying His commands. Remember this . . . for we will be held accountable! God does not want our sacrifice. **God wants OBEDIENCE!**

There is a chorus that says:

Obedience is the very best way
To show that you believe
Doing exactly what the Lord commands
Doing it happily.
Action is the key to obediency
Joy you will receive
Obedience is the very best way
To show that you believe.
O-B-E-D-I-E-N-C-E
Obedience is the very best way
To show that you believe!

God, in His Word, reminds us:

If ye love me,
keep my commandments.

(John 14:15)

We should not be swayed by the fragile wisdom of man. One must recognize that there are some popular men in the religious field who are seen on television frequently. Their influence is great but they compromise the Gospel, allowing many to go astray. They will be held accountable for their actions. And we should not follow them. God tells us, in His Word through His servant, Peter:

We ought to obey God rather than men.

(Acts 5:29)

B. In following God

While we may agree to obey God's Word, we sometimes find it difficult to follow God for this requires what appears to us to be sacrifices on our part.

Yet Jesus reminds us:

> . . .*If any man will come after Me,*
> *let him deny himself,*
> *and take up his cross,*
> *and follow Me.*
>
> (Matthew 16:24)

In Luke 18:18-25 we see how riches can become a stumbling block in following God. The rich young ruler was not willing to make the sacrifice for service.

In your own life, it may not be riches which are standing between you and God. It may be possessions. It may be power. It may be prestige. Whatever it is, confess the sin and determine with God's help to follow Him. You will be held accountable!

C. In imitating God

To imitate God is to seek to follow the example of God, to act the same as, to use God as our pattern, our model.

It is best reflected in the last part of the verse which reads:

> . . .*Christ* **in you,** *the hope of glory.*
> (Colossians 1:27)

There is depth of treasure in this verse with far reaching blessing. A book could be written on this verse alone! In a sense, our life should be so in tune with God in obedience that we become an extension of Christ . . . Christ **IN** us!

Some guidance and light on this theme is found in Ephesians 4:32:

> . . . be ye kind one to another,
> tenderhearted,
> forgiving one another.
> even as God for Christ's sake
> hath forgiven you.

Again, we will be held accountable for how faithfully we imitate God!

Attitude Of Praise

What should our attitude be towards God?

> The angels praised Him
> (Revelation 5:11, 12)
> The shepherds praised Him
> (Luke 2:20)
> The disciples praised Him
> (Luke 19:37).

Surely, then, our attitude should be one of constant praise!

> And my tongue shall speak
> of Thy righteousness
> and of Thy praise
> all the day long!
> (Psalm 35:28)

Self-centered Praying

How often do you thank the Lord? I do not mean . . . how often do you thank Him for what you feel are real answers to prayer! I hope you can grasp the significance of this! I call this self-centered thankfulness.

Here are some examples:

1. You pray for a raise in pay.
2. You pray for healing from sickness.
3. You pray for a new home.
4. You pray for a better car.
5. You pray for financial security.

These may be individually fine—but they are all self-centered prayers. Some may be answered. And when they are, you offer a prayer of thanks and gratitude. In themselves, they are not wrong. But the danger lies in the fact that most often, they are the only prayers we offer!

Honestly now, how often have you prayed:

1. Lord, thank you for dying for my sins.
2. Lord, thank you for sending the rain.
3. Lord, thank you for the testings and trials.
4. Lord, thank you for my financial insecurity.
5. Lord, thank you for giving me another day to serve You!

When our attitude towards God changes, our life changes!

Why shall "... my tongue ... speak of Thy righteousness and of Thy Praise all the day long" (Psalm 35:28)?

Look at the verse which precedes this:

> Let the Lord be magnified,
> which hath pleasure
> in the prosperity
> of His servant!

(Psalm 35:27)

**Prosperity
In
Poverty!**

If, then our attitude is one of gratitude towards God . . . what will happen? We shall prosper! That prosperity is not measured by man's standards (financial security, perpetual happiness in this world, etc.). That propserity is measured by God's standards. And that is quite different. Do you believe that there can be prosperity in poverty? Of course! Can there be prosperity in trials? YES! Read James 1:2–4.

What is your name?

My name is Christian.

Are you living like one . . . Scripturally? If not, is it not time to change your attitude!

✓ CHECKLIST FOR SPIRITUAL GROWTH

My Attitude Towards God

If "No" . . . where do I stand spiritually, right now?

1. When problems or questions occur in my daily life, do I follow the Scriptures faithfully in the answer to that problem?

   YES ☐ | NO ☐   Totally Lacking ☐   Needs Improving ☐

2. Am I always willing to forgive an individual who I feel has wronged me . . . and not carry a grudge?

   YES ☐ | NO ☐   Totally Lacking ☐   Needs Improving ☐

3. Is my daily praying Christ-centered and not self-centered?

   YES ☐ | NO ☐   Totally Lacking ☐   Needs Improving ☐

4. Do I thank God daily for His multiple blessings to me?

   YES ☐ | NO ☐   Totally Lacking ☐   Needs Improving ☐

If you have checked the TOTALLY LACKING Box . . . it means that, in this specific category . . . spiritually . . . you are failing. You need to realign your priorities . . . and strive for spiritual growth, now!

If you checked NEEDS IMPROVEMENT Box . . . it means that you are striving for a fulfilled Christian life . . . but recognize your need to make further improvements.

As a believer, God's measure of blessing and answered prayer in your life will be directly proportionate to your full obedience to His Word.

3

OUR ATTITUDE TOWARDS OTHERS

As believers, we are held accountable as to how we express our anger. It must be an anger with a <u>righteous,</u> holy cause. It must be an anger <u>without malice</u> (evil intent).

* * *

When angry for a righteous cause, it is important that we "... let not the sun go down upon your wrath" (Ephesians 4:26).

* * *

Our conversation should be one that builds up the hearer rather than tears down. For in corrupt conversation we simply, by slander, give place to the devil. See Ephesians 4:27.

* * *

As believers, we must daily remind ourself, that we are to be held accountable for our conversation. Upon entering church on Sunday, is our conversation frivolous and empty chatter or is it preparing us to worship a holy God?

* * *

Quarrelling is a weakness of the flesh and reveals a carnal Christian (James 4:1,2). How often a home can be wrecked because one member harbors a resentment that evidences itself in a quarrelsome spirit!

* * *

How often do we exercise more kindness to friends and even to total strangers than we do to immediate members of our family! This is wrong! Our kindness must be universal ... with love beginning **first** at home.

3

OUR ATTITUDE TOWARDS OTHERS

**Learn
To Say
"Thank You"**

There is a familiar chorous we often sing:

Jesus
Others
and
You

What a wonderful way to spell JOY!

How many times it becomes just a song and fails to become part of our automatic life style as believers in Christ! We become so self-centered that we don't even express gratitude to others who have helped us along life's way.

You will recall that Joseph, while in Pharaoh's prison, interpreted the dream of the chief butler. Joseph asked that the butler remember him to the Pharaoh when he was released. But the Bible tells us:

*Yet did not the chief butler
remember Joseph,
but forgot him.*

(Genesis 40:23)

Joash (Jehoash), saved from the murderous orgy of Athaliah, was sheltered for six years by his uncle Jehoida. Upon Jehoida's death, Joash became angry with Zechariah because he called out the sins of the nation Israel. Zechariah was Jehoida's son. Joash had him stoned to death in the temple court. The Bible records sadly:

> Thus Joash the king
> remembered not the kindness
> which Jehoida his father
> (the father of Zechariah)
> had done to him,
> but slew his son.
>
> (2 Chronicles 24:22)

(Later Joash's own servants murdered him while he lay sick. No mercy to him that showed no mercy—2 Chronicles 24:25.)

Guidelines For Growth

What are some of the Scriptural guidelines that should direct us in our attitude toward others? Many of them are found in Ephesians 4:25–31. I must admit as I read this that I am sometimes guilty of these very things. Improvements are needed in my own personal life . . . and yours! Here they are:

The Sin of Omission

A. <u>Stop lying to each other</u>
<u>(Ephesians 4:25)</u>
Often we tend to think of lying as simply telling an untruth. But some newspaper reporters and television commentators

Athaliah's Ruthless Rise To Power

Athaliah, Jezebel's daughter, was not going to let anything stand in her way to secure the throne. She slaughtered her own grandchildren . . . such was her greed for gain.

Sometimes, we have a tendency to generalize and grade sins. We look at Athaliah's sin as horrendous without realizing that our sins may be just as bad. Let me give you an example. Athaliah wanted to reach the top. To do so, she killed her own flesh and blood. That is sin!

Yet, how many people do you know who today are striving to reach the top. To do so, they neglect their own family, their own children. While they have not committed physical murder, in God's eyes they have sinned—committing spiritual murder, as the children turn away from God. Those children, now being trained in the ways of the Lord while young, soon grow up to follow the same greed for material gains their parents sought after.

Have you examined your own goals in life?

are daily using a form of sophisticated lying in order to sway the public in a certain direction.

It is not that what they say is not true. It could be and often is. But, it is <u>what they leave out</u> that sways their story in the direction they desire. This is LYING! It is one thing to tell the truth. It is quite another thing to tell the WHOLE TRUTH.

I am reminded of the story of a ship's captain who reprimanded a sailor for his continual drinking habit. The captain recorded the sailor's misbehavior in the ship's log book.

The sailor, angry that his misdeeds had been recorded . . . gained access to the log book and inscribed:

The captain did not drink today!

It was true! Yet it carried an implication that was false! One might call it "sophisticated lying." It is a sin. And, in our attitude towards others, we will be held accountable!

B. Be angry yet sin not
(Ephesians 4:26)

Righteous Indignation

On the surface, this may seem like a contradiction. How can you be angry and yet not sin? Some feel it is wrong to be angry. However, there are circumstances under which it would be very wrong not to be angry.

Christ was angry when he saw the self-righteous Pharisees going in and out of the temple of God. He knew that some of them held mortgages on widows' homes, often foreclosing on them and throwing them into the street. These Pharisees cloaked their misdeeds with long prayers. See Matthew 23:14. Christ expressed His anger here. He also expressed His anger in Mark 3:5.

There is such a thing as righteous anger, or in another word: indignation. God expressed anger against:

Miriam and Aaron	Numbers 12:9–15
The Israelites	Numbers 11:1–10
Balaam	Numbers 22:21, 22
Moses	Deuteronomy 4:21, 22

Redeem The Time

Here are two guidelines for a Christian's anger:

1. We should be slow in anger.
   See Proverbs 14:17.
2. We should not sin in anger.
   See Ephesians 4:26.

There are times when I get angry. I hate to wait in line. I think it is a waste of time. I become righteously indignant if I have a 2 PM dental appointment and I am kept waiting till 2:30. It robs me of my time. And God tells me to *redeem the time,* Ephesians 5:16. The reason we are to redeem the time is because the days are evil. We can't be redeeming time if we are wasting it because of someone else's insensitivity to our holy calling! That really makes me angry! I get riled up just writing it right now! But in becoming angry, I also try to be a witness to that individual who is robbing me of my time.

Anger Without Malice

Other things make me angry. Inflation, as an example, and the continual excuse for everyone to raise prices. Today the U.S. Postal Department announced they are going to raise first class rates from 15¢ an ounce to 20¢. One congressman suggested it might be better to go to 25¢. That sounds like a round figure. Why in the world don't they just raise it to $1 an ounce and be done with it? Any raise is ill advised in my opinion. I think it is the wrong way to approach the basic root problem. And it makes me angry!

However, as believers we are held accountable as to how we express our anger. It must be an anger with a righteous, holy cause. It must be an anger without malice!

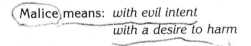

Malice means: *with evil intent*
with a desire to harm

This type of anger is wrong. It is sin. You will be held accountable for it. I am sure you can think of many personal illustrations where perhaps you have been the object of anger with evil intent. Or you, yourself, may have been guilty of this.

Anger is a wind which blows out the lamp of the mind. It is said that the Emperor Julius Caesar, when provoked, used to repeat the whole Roman alphabet before he permitted himself to speak. To disagree is one thing; to be disagreeable is another.

Is your marriage a wedlock or deadlock? Keep your eyes open before marriage . . . half shut afterwards. Remember, you can't express love with a clenched fist.

**Do Not
Go to
Bed
Angry!**

When angry for a righteous cause, it is important that we " . . . *let not the sun go down upon your wrath*" (Ephesians 4:26). This means, do not go to bed angry! A continued anger gives way to malice. And malice is sin. Verse 27 reminds us that continued anger only gives opportunity for the devil to get a foothold in your life!

In our anger toward others; it should be righteous anger only, it should not be with malice; it should not continue into the next day.

**How
Petty Feuds
Grow**

My wife and I knew a married couple who had a minor disagreement. They refused to speak to each other that day . . . and the next day . . . and the next day. This estrangement continued on for years. I doubt if they ever communicated with each other to their dying day. If you would have asked them what their original disagreement was . . . most likely, they would not have been able to recall it! What a shame.

To the pessiment . . .
life is just a pile of dirty dishes.

To the optimist . . .
life is a continuing banquet!

The Bible tells us: *"For anger and rage kill the foolish man; jealousy and indignation slay the simple"* (Job 5:2). How many times have you found that people whose constant attitude is one of envy and bitterness are often plagued with chronic illness!

What about your marriage? Are you communicating with your spouse? Or when a disagreement occurs, do you become strangely silent in your anger? If you do, don't let the sun go down upon your wrath!

Analyze your reasons for your anger with people. Is it due to some petty thing like:

> *I'm never asked to serve on the Mission Committee.*
>
> *Why didn't you take out the trash last night, like I asked you . . . 16 times?*
>
> *If you don't know what's wrong, John . . . well, I'm just not going to tell you!*
>
> *You know I don't like Okra, Helen! I'm going to McDonald's! Can't you learn to cook right!*

How petty in light of eternity! Take inventory of your attitude towards others in anger. You will be held accountable!

C. Say only what is good and helpful (Ephesians 4:29)

Be Positive In Speech

We are instructed in this verse to guard our conversation. It should not be corrupt that is, rotten or of a destroying nature. Rather, what we say should always be positive and uplifting. Our conversation should be one that builds up the hearer rather than tears down. For in corrupt conversation we simply, by slander, give place to the devil. See Ephesians 4:27.

The characteristics of a believer's conversation[1] should include the following.

1. Holy

As He which hath called you
is holy,
So be ye holy
in all manner
of conversation.

(1 Peter 1:15)

2. Honest

Having your conversation honest
. . . that, they may
by your good works,
which they shall behold
glorify God . . . .

(1 Peter 2:12)

3. Good

Having a good conscience;
that, whereas they speak
evil of you,
as of evildoers,
they may be ashamed
that falsely accuse
your good conversation
in Christ.

(1 Peter 3:16)

I know it is very easy, when we are falsely accused to snap back in bitter reply. It is much more difficult when you are held up in ridicule or slandered to return good conversation for evil. Yet, such action is a sign of spiritual maturity.

---

[1]The Greek word here translated by the King James Version as "con-versation" is anastrophe. This word refers to one's entire manner of life, including the outward expression of our speech—our "conversation."

**God's
Temple
Is Holy**

It is an attribute that I, myself, must be more diligent in. As believers, we must daily remind ourself, that we are to be held accountable for our conversation. Upon entering church on Sunday is our conversation frivolous and empty chatter or is it preparing us to worship a holy God? Is our daily conversation more directed to selfish, personal motives, or is it bathed in a holy purpose revealing our citizenship in Heaven?

This is how we will be held accountable!

D. Do not cause the Holy Spirit sorrow (Ephesians 4:30)

**Live Like
The Child
of a
King!**

If you are a child of God, then live like a child of God should live. To live otherwise grieves the Holy Spirit. If it causes the Holy Spirit to be sorry for your lifestyle, it also causes sorrow to God and Jesus Christ, the complete Trinity.

That which grieves the Holy Spirit is sin! The Holy Spirit will never leave the believer. We have been sealed by Him unto the day of redemption. See Ephesians 1:13, 14. For a practical example . . . it is possible for you to cause sorrow to your mother because of some wrong action in your life. However, she will not leave or forsake you. You are her son. She seals you with her continual love, regardless of the circumstance.

The Holy Spirit ministers constantly to us.

1. **He Guides Us**

   He will guide you into all truth.

   (John 16:13)

2. **He Empowers Us**

   *. . . I am full of power
   by the Spirit of the Lord.*

   (Micah 3:8)

3. **He Anoints Us**

   Because the Holy Spirit lives within you, you have someone to affirm to you what is right or wrong. God's Word illuminated by God's Holy Spirit is your final guide—not any man! What greater responsibility . . . because you know what is right . . . not to cause the Holy Spirit sorrow! See 1 John 2:27.

**Six
Attributes
Of the
Holy Spirit**

The Holy Spirit also Regenerates (John 3: 3, 5), Indwells (Romans 8:11), Baptizes (Acts 2:17–41), Sanctifies (Romans 15:16, 2 Thessalonians 2:13), gives Joy (Romans 14:17), and Comforts (John 14:16–26).

How we live not only affects others around us . . . it also can cause joy or grief to the Holy Spirit.

Our daily walk with the Holy Spirit is recorded by God. And we will be held accountable at the Judgment Seat of Christ!

E. Eliminate bitterness from your life
(Ephesians 4:31)

Sins
God
Hates

Someone once said: *"I love humanity. It's people I can't stand."* Admittedly, it can be difficult to love some people. That's a challenge I sometimes face.

In verse 31, we see some of the particular sins that do grieve the Holy Spirit. We tend to think of sin only in what we believe are grosser iniquities such as stealing, unfaithfulness or a capital crime. But listed in this verse are sins which God looks on as equal sins:

> Bitterness and wrath
> Anger
> Clamor (quarrelsome)
> Evil speaking

What are the root causes of such bitterness? Bitterness can be caused by:

1. Childlessness (1 Samuel 1:10)
2. Foolishness (Proverbs 17:25)
3. Sickness (Isaiah 38:17)
4. Sin (Proverbs 5:4)
5. Death (Jeremiah 31:15)
6. Envy (Romans 13:13)

Quarrelling
Reveals
Sin

Have you ever met a quarrelsome Christian? Quarrelling is a weakness of the flesh and reveals a carnal Christian (James 4:1, 2). How often a home can be wrecked because one member harbors a resentment that evidences itself in a quarrelsome spirit!

In 1967 I took my first round-the-world trip investigating world conditions. I remember flying into Amman, Jordan and driving outside the city to the barren desert. There, in the middle of nowhere was an Arab refugee camp.

The family pictured above had lost everything which represented about $2500 in property and goods. They asked me to sit down and drink Turkish coffee with them. I walked inside their tent to see what possessions they had brought with them. All I found were a couple pots and pans, a little coffee pot and four tiny coffee cups—from which they humbly served me.

I had eaten in opulent restaurants, spotlessly clean. But now, as the sand whipped across our faces . . . I felt at home. Here was humble truth unvarnished by the glittering selfishness of the world. I would not have traded that experience for anything.

They were homeless! Their material possessions were meager. Yet, in spite of the hoplessness of their situation . . . they exercised kindness!

Strive, therefore, to eliminate bitterness . . . all bitterness . . . from your heart. For, in harboring any shred of bitterness by way of malicious anger or quarrelling or evil speaking . . . you are grieving the Holy Spirit.

And you will be held accountable!

F. Be kind and forgiving (Ephesians 4:32)

Exercising Kindness

It was Dr. Henrietta C. Mears who said:

Kindness has converted more sinners than zeal, eloquence, or learning.

Kindness is a friendly and concerned attitude toward others. It could be said that there are **two** types of kindness.

1. **Natural kindness** (Acts 28:2)

   This was a kindness shown Paul by the people of Malta when shipwrecked. They exercised hospitality by building a fire to warm them from the cold rain. We should demonstrate such kindness even to total strangers.

2. **Acquired kindness** (Colossians 3 : 1 2)

   This is a specially motivated kindness—displayed by a Christian. Because we have been chosen of God and are the recipients of His love, we should practice the exercise of kindness towards others. In our new life in Christ, we need to acquire a deeper sense of kindness.

Love Begins At Home!

How often do we exercise more kindness to friends and even to total strangers than we do to immediate members of our family! This is wrong! Our kindness must be universal, with love beginning **first** at home.

Coupled with kindness, we must have a forgiving nature. This can be difficult. I can remember a millionaire who was a Christian who was ruthless in his dealings with others. One friend of mine, entrapped in this millionaire's business dealings, had to declare bankruptcy. Another close Christian friend similarly connected was so distressed by the way he, too, was treated, that he committed suicide. And I myself also had to declare bankruptcy. I can recall a warm summer day shortly after when I had no money. I called the millionaire and asked him please to release sufficient money so we could buy some groceries. He refused!

Because of his enormous wealth, he became popular with many churches and Christian organizations. Perhaps they felt that some of his wealth would rub off on them! His life story, outlining his meteoric rise to success, appeared in many publications. When he died suddenly, his funeral was attended by a host of well-known Christian personalities.

I admit that I was bitter and unforgiving for the way this man treated me and a host of others. But in the last few years I have tried to exercise the gift of forgiveness. This man had a vision. He helped many. He was not perfect. Unfortunately, I bore the brunt of some of his weaknesses . . . as did others. But God used him and in his later years, we became friends again in true Christian fellowship. My sin was in not being forgiving and committing it all to the Lord sooner—in fact, immediately.

If we are not forgiving . . . and forgetting (Philippians 3:13) . . . we shall be held accountable at the Judgment Seat of Christ!

✓ CHECKLIST FOR SPIRITUAL GROWTH

My Attitude Towards Others

If "No" ... where do I stand spiritually, right now?

1. Do I always seek to tell the truth and not try (by omitting certain facts) to commit the sin of omission?

   YES ☐ | NO ☐   Totally Lacking ☐   Needs Improving ☐

2. When I do get angry, is it a righteous anger without malice or evil intent?

   YES ☐ | NO ☐   Totally Lacking ☐   Needs Improving ☐

3. Do I always make it a point never to go to bed angry?

   YES ☐ | NO ☐   Totally Lacking ☐   Needs Improving ☐

4. Is my conversation always uplifting and one that builds up, rather than tears down?

   YES ☐ | NO ☐   Totally Lacking ☐   Needs Improving ☐

5. Have I learned the secret of eliminating bitterness from my life?

   YES ☐ | NO ☐   Totally Lacking ☐   Needs Improving ☐

If you have checked the TOTALLY LACKING Box ... it means that, in this specific category ... spiritually ... you are failing. You need to realign your priorities ... and strive for spiritual growth, now!

If you checked NEEDS IMPROVEMENT Box ... it means that you are striving for a fulfilled Christian life ... but recognize your need to make further improvements.

As a believer, God's measure of blessing and answered prayer in your life will be directly proportionate to your full obedience to His Word.

4

OUR PRAYER LIFE

If our Father knows in advance what we have need of, why then do we pray? We pray because God still wants us to ask Him and to depend on Him to meet our needs. We also pray so that we will better realize what our own needs are.

* * *

Prayer is not simply the vocal or silent petitioning of God with our requests.

* * *

Prayer is more important, an inner heart attitude of dependence upon God and true communion with God.

* * *

Our lives should be lived in an attitude of grateful prayer to God. Our outward walk reflects our inward prayer life.

4

OUR PRAYER LIFE

Praying With Purpose

I must confess my prayer life is not what it should be! In this busy world, we Christians simply do not take time to pray as we should. Oh, yes, we go through the perfunctory prayers. But, we too easily can fall into a routine of praying without meaning, praying without purpose . . . just because it is the thing to do.

One area of time we all have available for prayer is right before the service begins on Sunday morning in church. Often I try to get to church 15 or 20 minutes early to quietly commune with God. But this silence is often broken by sporadic chattering of those entering the sanctuary. We are guilty of not observing the holiness of God's house. And we will be held accountable!

Personal Requirements

God has given us some personal requirements we must fulfill when we pray. They include:

A. Praying with Purity of Heart

If I regard iniquity (sin)
in my heart,
The Lord will not hear me.
(Psalm 66:18)

B. Praying According to God's Will

. . . if we ask any thing
according to His will,
He heareth us.
(1 John 5:14)

C. Praying without Depending on Vain Repetitions.

. . . when we pray,
use not vain repetitions,
as the heathen do:
 for they think
 they shall be heard
 for their much speaking.

(and this is one of my favorite promises from God) . . .

for your Father knoweth
 what things we have need of,
before *we ask Him!*
(Matthew 6:7, 8)

Why Pray?

If our Father knows in advance what we have need of, why then do we pray? Why then is it our responsibility to pray?

We pray because God still wants us to ask Him and to depend on Him to meet our needs. We also pray so that we will better realize what our own needs are. We also pray in knowledge of these needs . . .

Does God answer our prayers?

Yes! **(1)** Beyond our expectation (Jeremiah 33:3); **(2)** Sometimes after delay (Luke 18:7); **(3)** Sometimes differently from our desire (2 Corinthians 12:8, 9); **(4)** Sometimes immediately (Isaiah 65:24). Our prayer is not answered if we ask amiss (James 4:3).

How To Pray Triumphantly!

Many believers think of prayer as a time to ask God for things we want. Perhaps that's why some of our prayers go unanswered. Someone has suggested this guideline for effective prayer.

A doration
First praise God in worship and love.
C onfession
Then confess your sins to Him.
T hanksgiving
Thank Him for every blessing of the day.
S upplication
Finally, let your requests be made known.

You will find this prayer life will change your daily walk with God and give you victory.

God Answers Your Prayers When You Meet His Standard

The key to praying Scripturally is found in John 15:7. Many people become disappointed in praying because they read Matthew 21:22 which is the **Promise** but do not receive the answer they want because they have not fulfilled the **Condition.** Read John 15:7, quoted below.

If ye abide in Me Abide means to dwell continually in the very presence of God . . . not just on Sundays from 11 to 12 or when an emergency exists.

And My Words abide in you By constantly abiding in Christ, you will want to do the will of the Father. Your life daily, by example, will reflect God's every abiding presence. This will give you a new perspective on your prayer requests. Your walk must reflect your talk (your testimony).

Ye shall ask what ye will Your prayer requests, in light of your abiding in Christ and living a dedicated Christian life, will be reappraised by you. Those things that you once thought important prayer requests will fade into insignificance.

And it shall be done unto you. Following the 3 steps above, faithfully, God will answer every prayer request without fail . . . not always to your earthly planning, but most certainly, for your eternal good, *"No good thing will He withhold from them that walk uprightly"* (Psalm 84:11). *"Your Father knoweth what things ye have need of,* **before** *ye ask Him"* (Matthew 6:8).

trusting God to meet our needs. It is constantly taking spiritual inventory of our life . . . so that Christ truly is IN us and our life is in HIM!

And here comes a verse which, on the surface, seems impossible to fulfill:

Pray without ceasing.
(1 Thessalonians 5:17)

Begin the Day with Prayer

Every morning it is my usual custom to drive to a local restaurant for a small breakfast. This gives me opportunity to read the morning newspaper so I can keep abreast of world activities in light of Bible prophecy. It is about a 15 minute ride. In the past, I would listen to a Christian radio station or a cassette.

I found my day was much more enriched when, instead, I would spend this driving time in earnest prayer . . . seeking God's guidance for the day, presenting my needs and taking to Him my concerns. With all things in His hands, I found nervous tension disappeared, and a calm assurance blanketed my day.

How do you pray without ceasing?

Paul in 1 Thessalonians 1:3 also states that he was *"Remembering without ceasing your work of faith . . . ."*

An Inner Heart Attitude

Prayer is not simply the vocal or silent petitioning of God with our requests. What is even more important, is an inner heart attitude of dependence upon God and true communion with God.

Our family, particularly those away from home, are constantly in our prayers. Pictured above is our son-in-law, Wes Frick with our daughter, Doreen. Their children *(left to right)* are Jessica, Piper, Joel and Joshua. They live in Washington state.

We are always, as Paul did, remembering those we love. My wife and I have a daughter, Doreen, who is married and lives some 3000 miles away near Spokane, Washington. She and her husband and family are always hidden in our heart. We are not always talking about them. But our love daily goes out to them. We remember them.

Likewise, we are not always praying. We pray daily at some set intervals and also at various unset times during the day . . . as the Lord leads. But our lives should be lived in an attitude of grateful prayer to God. In that sense . . . our daily walk is an unceasing prayer life if we are IN Christ and Christ is IN us! Thus, our outward walk reflects our inward prayer life.

And we will be held accountable for our prayer life!

✓ CHECKLIST FOR SPIRITUAL GROWTH

My Prayer Life

If "No" ... where do I stand spiritually, right now?

	YES	NO	Totally Lacking	Needs Improving
1. Do I begin each morning with prayer?	☐	☐	☐	☐
2. Before Church service begins on a Sunday, do I spend these few moments in communion with God?	☐	☐	☐	☐
3. Is my daily life lived in an attitude of prayer? Do I pray in those spare moments ... while driving, waiting for an appointment, etc.?	☐	☐	☐	☐
4. In my prayer life, do my prayers first begin with **A**doration, **C**onfession and **T**hanksgiving?	☐	☐	☐	☐
5. In my prayer life, do I **first** pray for others and my own personal needs last?	☐	☐	☐	☐

If you have checked the TOTALLY LACKING Box ... it means that, in this specific category ... spiritually ... you are failing. You need to realign your priorities ... and strive for spiritual growth, now!

If you checked NEEDS IMPROVEMENT Box ... it means that you are striving for a fulfilled Christian life ... but recognize your need to make further improvements.

As a believer, God's measure of blessing and answered prayer in your life will be directly proportionate to your full obedience to His Word.

5
OUR PRIORITIES

A believer must learn to discipline himself to do the things in the order of importance.

* * *

God's Word tells us to live one day at a time. God will take care of tomorrow just as He has taken care of today.

* * *

The duties of a Christian include: **(1)** Giving ourselves to God (Romans 12:1) and **(2)** Living a transforming life (Romans 12:2). If our life is not transformed, our priorities will be self-centered, not God-centered.

* * *

If you are spiritually grounded, you will recognize what activities are self-centered and not God-centered. Our priorities will reveal our degree of obedience to Him.

5

OUR PRIORITIES

Realign Priorities

A believer must learn to discipline himself to do things in the order of importance.

Honestly examine your own priorities in life. Do you find yourself worrying about:

A. Your Life

> *Be not anxious for your life . . .*
> (Matthew 6:25)

B. Your Clothing

> *Why are you anxious for raiment?*
> *Consider the lilies of the field,*
> *how they grow;*
> *they toil not,*
> *neither do they spin . . .*
>
> *If God so clothe*
> *the grass of the field . . .*
> *shall He not much more*
> *clothe you, O ye of little faith?*
> (Matthew 6:28, 30)

C. Your Food

> *Be not anxious saying,*
> *What shall we eat . . .*
>
> *. . . yet have I not seen*
> *the righteous forsaken,*
> *nor his seed begging bread.*
> (Matthew 6:31; Psalm 37:25)

D. Your Future

> *Take no thought for the morrow . . .*
> (Matthew 6:34)

**Live
One Day
At a Time!**

Unfortunately, too often we find our thoughts and our actions pre-occupied with our own personal life, striving to earn an income to stay on our standard of living, to provide food and clothing in keeping with our life style. Besides this, we are concerned about the future . . . particularly tomorrow. Yet God's Word tells us to live one day at a time. God will take care of tomorrow just as He has taken care of today.

Our priorities are backwards. Instead of placing God first in our daily priority, we place family and self first; then fit in God if there is room. This is wrong. It is sin. And we will be held accountable. If we place God first, concentrating on spiritual values, and resting in His confidence . . . God, who knows our temporal needs, will supply what is necessary for each day!

**A Heart
Knowledge**

How we are so often guilty of a head knowledge of God's providence but not a heart knowledge.

It is God's will that I should cast
My care on Him each day (1 Peter 5:7).

He also asks me not to cast
My confidence away (Hebrews 10:35).

But, oh, how foolishly I act
When taken unaware . . .
I cast away my confidence
And carry all my care!

Above are **ALL** the material possessions you will be able to take with you when you die!

NONE!

Where are you devoting all your energy, your time and your money? Be honest in answering this question. Perhaps it is time to realign your priorities emphasizing those priorities that are beyond price and that are enduring.

The duties of a Christian include:

1. Giving Ourselves to God

> . . . *present your bodies*
> *a living sacrifice,*
> *holy,*
> *acceptable to God*
> *which is your reasonable service.*
> (Romans 12:1)

2. A Transforming Life

> *Be not conformed to this world:*
> *but be ye transformed*
> *by the renewing of your mind . . . .*
> (Romans 12:2)

While it is necessary for us to be in the world, we are not to be of the world. We should not take on the style of the external things of the world that would water down our ministry for our Lord and Saviour. If our life is not transformed, our priorities will be self-centered, not God-centered.

Questionable Motives

I receive the distinct impression that many people attend church on Sundays simply to fulfill an obligation. There is a tendency for some to simply go through the motions. To ease our conscience we help sponsor a missionary, give to the building fund or to a special project.

Some churches even devote one Sunday a year to *"Sacrificial Sunday."* On this Sunday, individuals are supposed to give "sacrificially" in the offering.

It has been said:

Generally when a man climbs to success, a woman is holding the ladder.

Women have:

A smile for every joy,
A tear for every sorrow,
A consolation for every grief,
An excuse for every fault,
A prayer for every misfortune,
Encouragement for every hope.

Too often, women are the workhorse both in the local church and on the mission field, but are not given the credit they deserve.

Paul, in Romans 16:3, remembers Priscilla and her husband Aquila and in verse 4 recalls that they risked their lives for him.

Priscilla, a Jewess who had come out of Italy with her husband to live at Corinth and about 18 months later at Ephesus, . . . was one of the most influential women in the New Testament Church.

Priscilla not only managed her household and worked at tent making—possibly by weaving the cloth—but she also found time to be a thorough student of the Gospel of Jesus Christ.

Priscilla was not only a woman of attainment but one willing to make sacrifices in the spreading of the gospel, for she lived at a time when a Christian faced great persecution. But Priscilla was not afraid!

And Paul says of Priscilla and Aquila that not only does he owe them a debt of gratitude but "*. . . also all the churches of the Gentiles*" (vs. 4).

Priscilla and Aquila were WORTHY TO BE COUNTED.

Will the Lord Jesus Christ be able to say this of you? Examine your own life . . . right now. What are you doing for Christ that will **count?** If your list is short, there is still time to remedy the situation. And by so doing your life will be so much more full and meaningful.

God-Centered Goals

I challenge you to mark down each activity you do for the next week. The chart on the next page will guide you in this.

You will soon see very vividly where your priorities are. This does not mean that every minute of every day must be taken up with reading the Bible or witnessing or praying.

God-centered responsibilities would include:

As a woman . . .

A. Preparing nutritious meals for your family.

B. Praying for their emotional and physical needs.

C. Showing love and devotion to your husband.

D. Fulfilling, as unto God, your responsible duties.

God has given women many responsible roles. None can be a greater missionary field for a wife than that of her own family!

DISCOVERING LIFE'S TRUE VALUES

MY MATERIAL POSSESSIONS

(List items of material value here such as Clothes - $450, Automobile - $3500, Camera - $70, Furniture - $5200, House, Hobby and Sport equipment, Bank Account, Insurance, etc.)

On this side, list items of material value you *now* possess and estimate their dollar value.

On this side, list items of material value you are striving or desire to possess (such as: New Job, Promotion, New Car, Television Set, Golf Clubs, Refrigerator, Bedroom Set, Rugs, etc.)

ITEMS I NOW POSSESS		ITEMS I DESIRE TO POSSESS	
ITEM	$ VALUE	ITEM	$ VALUE
1. House	$	1.	$
2. Automobile		2.	
3. Furniture		3.	
4. Clothing		4.	
5. Television		5.	
6. Savings Account		6.	
7. Investments		7.	
8.		8.	
9.		9.	
10.		10.	
11.		11.	
12.		12.	
13.		13.	
14.		14.	
15.		15.	
TOTAL VALUE $		TOTAL VALUE $	
		$	

Do not be afraid when a man becomes rich, When the glory of his house is increased; For when he dies he will carry nothing away; His glory will not descend after him. (Psalm 49:16-17)

DISCOVERING LIFE'S TRUE VALUES

POSSESSIONS
MONEY CANNOT BUY

On a Marking Scale of 1 to 3, grade your estimate of achievement in accumulating possessions that money cannot buy.

Place a **1** under Sale of Achievement if you have **not** achieved this goal. Place a **2** under Scale of Achievement if you **occasionally** achieve this goal. Place a **3** under Scale of Achievement if you have **successfully** achieved this goal.

POSSESSIONS MONEY CANNOT BUY   Scale of Achievement

1. Eternal Life, (John 3:16; Romans 6:23; 10:9)

2. Harmony in Your Home

3. A Fulfilled Happy Marriage

4. Love and Respect from your Children

5. Family Devotions

6. Personal Morning and Evening Devotions

7. Attend Church Faithfully

8. The ability to say: "I'm sorry."

9. The ability to say: "I made a mistake."

10. Peace of Mind

11. Abundant Health

12. Freedom from Fear

13. Freedom from Worry

14. Exhibit Joy through Trials

15. A Thankful Happy Heart

Total Scale of Achievement ➡

40 - 45	You have discovered Life's true values!
35 - 39	You are making progress. Check your weak points and strive to bring them up to Scale 3 level.
25 - 34	You need to realign your priorities in life. Are you seeking the best of both worlds? You can't serve two masters! Honestly appraise your life's direction and plan to change your priorities.
Under 25	You should very seriously reexamine your life and your goals in light of eternal values. Your priorities are misappropriated. Make major changes now while you still have time.

God-centered responsibilities would include:

As a man . . .

A. Earning an income to meet basic family needs.

B. Daily guiding your family in a time of devotions at the Family Altar.

C. Showing by your life, leadership that exemplifies Christ.

D. Showing love and care for your wife and family.

Self-centered Activities

Some activities that could become self-centered activities include:

A. Playing golf or some other sport.

B. Serving on several school or church committees.

C. Attending too many outside functions whether they be social or church-oriented.

D. Paying more attention to your hobby rather than your hubby.

E. Working overtime or holding down two jobs.

F. Overindulging in eating.

Run That Ye Might Obtain

Nearing the finish line at a University of Pennsylvania race, one runner totally exhausted fell flat on his face, short of the final goal.

Paul reminds us, in 1 Corinthians 9:24, 25, that a Christian should not run his race aimlessly. Nor does he waste his time. We should give up pleasures of this world that **occupy time** but are unproductive in the Christian race of service to Jesus Christ. Are you running so you might obtain eternal crowns?

You will know what activities are self-centered and not God-centered, if you are spiritually grounded in the Word.

If your attitude is:

> *Why can't I go to the motion pictures once in a while?*
>
> *Why can't I listen to Christian rock music?*
>
> *What's wrong with an occasional glass of wine or beer?*
>
> *Why can't I go to the football game? They only have it on Sunday.*

then, it is obvious that your Christianity is just a convenient self-centered surface theology to ease your conscience.

Christ gave His life so that we might have eternal life (John 3:16).

Our priorities will reveal our degree of obedience to Him.

Christ will measure it by our faithfulness and fruitfulness. Read John 15:1–6.

By these measures . . . we will be held accountable at the Judgment Seat of Christ!

✓ CHECKLIST FOR SPIRITUAL GROWTH

My Priorities

If "No" ... where do I stand spiritually, right now?

1. Have I learned the secret of living one day at a time, resting wholly on the Lord?

   YES ☐ | NO ☐ | Totally Lacking ☐ | Needs Improving ☐

2. Instead of worrying, do I cast <u>all</u> my burdens on the Lord ... and leave them there!

   YES ☐ | NO ☐ | Totally Lacking ☐ | Needs Improving ☐

3. Do I faithfully go to Church on Sunday because I love to commune with God fellowshipping with other believers?

   YES ☐ | NO ☐ | Totally Lacking ☐ | Needs Improving ☐

   (If you go because everyone else does or simply to meet your friends ... then you should check the "No" block).

If you have checked the TOTALLY LACKING Box ... it means that, in this specific category ... spiritually ... you are failing. You need to realign your priorities ... and strive for spiritual growth, now!

If you checked NEEDS IMPROVEMENT Box ... it means that you are striving for a fulfilled Christian life ... but recognize your need to make further improvements.

As a believer, God's measure of blessing and answered prayer in your life will be directly proportionate to your full obedience to His Word.

6

OUR MOTIVES

Motives are our inner impulse which produces outward action.

* * *

We may do all the right things in our attitude towards <u>God,</u> in our attitude towards <u>others,</u> in our <u>prayer life,</u> in our <u>priorities</u> and still come up on the minus side in our fruitfulness to God. Why? Because our basic motives in doing all these things may be self-centered.

* * *

Many people seek Christ not as Saviour but as Santa Claus! They seek to gain acceptance, popularity, financial success or physical healing. Their motives are wrong.

6

OUR MOTIVES

Misdirected Motives

We may do all the right things in our attitude towards God, in our attitude towards others, in our prayer life, in our priorities and still come up on the minus side in our fruitfulness to God. At the Judgment Seat of Christ, we may discover that we receive only few rewards.

Why?

Because of our basic motives in doing all these things! Motives are our inner impulse which produces outward action.

I am reminded of the little girl who came to the dinner table with dirty hands. Her mother told her to wash her hands and sit in the corner for 5 minutes. At the end of that time she was invited to join the family at dinner, if she had learned her lesson.

The little girl sat at the table, piously folded her hands and prayed:

Lord, Thou preparest a table before me in the presence of mine enemies.

While she knew it was proper to thank the Lord for the food, her motive for quoting Psalm 23:5 was not one borne out of love.

You will recall Haman's plans backfired because they had evil motives and intent behind them. See Esther 6:6–11.

Peter's motives in doubting the necessity of the crucifixion were prompted by Satan (Matthew 16:22, 23).

Ananias and Sapphira, his wife, had motives which were not God-centered but self-centered. Their outward display in contributing to the church did not deceive Peter. They paid the penalty of sudden death for their deception. See Acts 5:1–11.

Many a good thing is done with a wrong motive. Be sure to read John 6:26.

Christ Is Not A Santa Claus!

Many people seek Christ not as Saviour but as Santa Claus! Do you? They seek Christ to gain acceptance, popularity, financial success, physical healing. Their motives are wrong—they have often been ill advised, and lured to follow Christianity for this world's rewards. Love-directed motives help us realize that we are called to suffer with Christ (Romans 8:17). For in suffering with Him, we shall reign with Him (2 Timothy 2:12).

Our *"motive"* is our inner drive or intention that causes us to do something or act in a certain way.

Too often, as believers, our motives for following Christ are misdirected or not God-centered. Jesus saw this when after He had fed the 5000 . . . some followed Him across the Sea of Galilee to Capernaum.

Knowing their mis-directed motives, Jesus told them:

> *Ye seek Me,*
> *not because ye saw the miracles,*
> *but because*
> *ye did eat of the loaves,*
> *and were filled.*
>
> (John 6:26)

In Acts 5:1-16, we see another example of misdirected motives. In New Testament days believers often shared their wealth with other believers. It was purely **voluntary.**

Ananias and his wife Sapphira owned some land, which they sold. The money which they gained from this sale was theirs to keep and use as they pleased!

The sin of Ananias was not in keeping back this money . . . but, rather, in his pretending a complete consecration to God while deliberately keeping back part of the money. In other words, Ananias pretended that the part they handed over to the church was the whole of the sale!

This was a sin of insincere consecration, for it meant lying to God! Sapphira (means *beautiful*) had knowledge of this deception. God's judgment for dishonest motives was instant death! See Acts 5:5, 10.

In your service to Christ . . . **what are your motives?** Are they God-centered or self-centered?

Take inventory in your motives for teaching Sunday School, for serving as an elder or deacon, for dating a certain boy or girl, for serving on a committee. If your motives are self-directed . . . pray, seeking God's grace to help you make them Christ-directed.

For you will be held accountable at the Judgment Seat of Christ!

✓CHECKLIST FOR SPIRITUAL GROWTH

My Motives

If "No" ... where do I stand spiritually, right now?

1. Do I daily serve Christ because of His love for me and His sacrifice on Calvary so that I might have eternal life?

   YES ☐   NO ☐   Totally Lacking ☐   Needs Improving ☐

   (If you serve Christ to gain acceptance, to seek financial success, physical healing or popularity ... then your motives are wrong. You should check the "No" block.)

2. Have I accepted Christ because my girlfriend (or boyfriend) has demonstrated by her life ideal Christian standards that I seek to strive for?

   YES ☐   NO ☐   Totally Lacking ☐   Needs Improving ☐

   (If you accepted Christ simply to satisfy your saved girlfriend or boyfriend ... then your motives are wrong. You should check the "No" block.)

3. Am I serving God in my Church as an Elder, Deacon, Sunday School teacher, etc. willingly because of Christ's love for me at Calvary?

   YES ☐   NO ☐   Totally Lacking ☐   Needs Improving ☐

   (If your motives are self-directed or you are serving simply out of obligation or duty ... then your motives are wrong. You should check the "No" block.)

If you have checked the TOTALLY LACKING Box ... it means that, in this specific category ... spiritually ... you are failing. You need to realign your priorities ... and strive for spiritual growth, now!

If you checked NEEDS IMPROVEMENT Box ... it means that you are striving for a fulfilled Christian life ... but recognize your need to make further improvements.

As a believer, God's measure of blessing and answered prayer in your life will be directly proportionate to your full obedience to His Word.

7

OUR STEWARDSHIP OF TIME

Eternally speaking, our time on earth is but a brief moment! How, then, shall we live this time . . . for self or for the Saviour?

* * *

It's not the quantity of time we spend for the Lord . . . it's the quality of time. There is a big difference.

* * *

How sad that Americans have more time-saving devices and less time than any other people in the world. They plan for their future on earth as though time will stand still . . . yet they drive as though time is swiftly running out!

* * *

God reminds us that we are to redeem the time (Ephesians 5:16).

7

OUR STEWARDSHIP OF TIME

**Stewardship
More Than
Money**

Too often when we think of stewardship we relate it only to money. However, stewardship implies much, much more. As believers in Christ, our stewardship responsibilities are clearly spelled out. God, through His Son, Jesus Christ, has entrusted us with eternal life. That benefit and blessing begins the very moment we accept Christ as Lord and Saviour of our life. We are expected to use this trust profitably while on earth.

As a wise steward our life can no longer follow the ordinary lusts of men . . . earthly desires. Our actions must reflect a heavenly calling seeking daily the will of God (1 Peter 4:1, 2).

**Don't
Give God
Your
Spare Time**

Stewardship of TIME

Eternally speaking, our time on earth is but a brief moment. How, then, shall we live this time . . . for self or for the Saviour?

The Lord wants our precious time,
not our spare time!

How sad that Americans have more time-saving devices and less time than any other people in the world. They plan for their future on earth as though time will stand still, yet they drive as though time is swiftly running out!

It's not the quantity of time we spend for the Lord . . . it's the quality of time. There is a big difference.

**Wrong
Use
Of Time**

You can spend hours each week at your church on the kitchen committee or devote many hours each week travelling preaching the Gospel away from home. From a quantitative standpoint, you have devoted many hours in the Lord's work. But, if that time is misdirected, if the motives are wrong, if you by so doing are neglecting your family . . . the quality of that time is questionable!

Again . . . if you are on the mission field. If you are spending 5 hours a day in social services, or in teaching in a secular school, or arts and crafts . . . the quantity of time is there . . . but the quality of your time may be questionable!

How Do We Invest Our Time?

Two sisters lived in a quiet village on the southeast of the Mount of Olives, beside the Jericho Road. The town was Bethany. The two sisters were Mary and Martha.

Although they were sisters, they had two quite different personalities. Mary, it seems, had never married. She was compassionate and imaginative. She did not allow ordinary household chores to control her life.

Martha, on the other hand, was the homemaker. She strove for perfection around the house. When Jesus came to visit them, Mary immediately sat at His feet in worshipful adoration. But Martha, like a buzzing bee, was more concerned with household details than with a quiet moment of devotion.

In Luke 10:40 we read that Martha was distracted with all her preparations and she came up to Jesus and said, in effect, *"Lord, do You not care that my sister has left me to do all the serving alone? Then tell her to help me."*

Our Lord answered: *"Martha, Martha, thou art careful and troubled* (worried and bothered) *about many things: But one thing is needful: and Mary hath chosen that good part, which shall not be taken away from her"* (10:41, 42).

Both Mary and Martha witnessed Jesus raise their brother Lazarus from the dead. And six days before the Passover . . . the last feast attended by Jesus at Bethany . . . Martha again was probably busy in the kitchen. But it was Mary, because of her deep abiding love for her Saviour, who took a pound of very costly perfume valued at about $60 in those days ($250 today) and poured it on the feet of Jesus.

There are many Marthas today who strive for earthly perfection, sometimes at the cost of spiritual leanness. They allow little things in life . . . moles . . . to become mountains. Their life is one of constant, nervous energy . . . busy doing everything. If you are a Martha, stewing over everything, try to calm down and keep in mind our Lord's Words in Luke 10:41.

It is important, that as Christians, we live a balanced life. Certainly, we must not be *". . . so heavenly minded that we are no earthly good!"*

On the other hand, we must realize that simply being *"active"* in the Lord's work (attending Church services, serving on committees, planning banquets, etc.) is not a measure of our highest devotion for our Saviour. **Read John 6:27!**

**Valued
Advice**

In the 1920's a wealthy industrialist asked a friend how he could get more things accomplished in his business. The friend, a management consultant, suggested that each night he:

1. List all the things he wanted to do the following day . . . in any order, as they came to mind.

2. Then go down that list and number each planned activity in its order of productive importance, 1, 2, 3, etc.

3. Then, on that day, faithfully tackle each job in the order sequence noted. Do the first item of importance first. Don't get side-tracked. Continue on this first item until you have completely finished it.

   Then do the second item of importance from your previously prepared list.

   If there are 5 items on your list and you only accomplish the first two items . . . that's fine. Don't worry about it.

4. That evening, prepare another list and number each planned activity in the order of its productive importance.

The management consultant said to his business tycoon friend . . . *"Those are my suggestions. You and your administrative staff try this simple plan for 30 days. Then you can pay me whatever you feel it is worth."*

FORMULA FOR SUCCESS

THINGS I WANT TO ACCOMPLISH TOMORROW ...

List on this side the items you would like to accomplish tomorrow. Don't worry about their order or priority. Simply list them as they come to your mind.

1. _____
2. _____
3. _____
4. _____
5. _____
6. _____
7. _____

The Lord wants our precious time, not our spare time. The best use of time is to invest it in those things that will outlast it! One today is worth a dozen tomorrows!

"Redeeming the time, because the days are evil" (Ephesians 5:16).

FORMULA FOR SUCCESS

LISTED IN ORDER OF *PRODUCTIVE* IMPORTANCE . . .

On this side . . . list the items you would like to accomplish tomorrow. HOWEVER, list them in order of their *productive* importance . . . keeping eternity's values in view.

Then . . . without fail . . . tackle the **first** item on your list that day . . . and **complete it!** Then . . . go to the **second** item on your list. Then, if you have time . . . tackle the **third** item on your list. Do not skip around or over any item simply because you would prefer to do the easiest or most enjoyable first.

Don't worry about those jobs on the list you could not get to. You may wish to place them on tomorrow's list. At least, you have accomplished that day those items of most productive importance. **And that's the secret to successful living!**

1. _____

2. _____

3. _____

4. _____

5. _____

6. _____

7. _____

". . . seek ye first the kingdom of God and His righteousness; and all these things shall be added unto you" (Matthew 6:33).

Remember, this was in the 1920's. The industrialist put the plan to work for 30 days. He was so impressed by the success of this tithing of TIME that he handed his friend a check for $25,000!

Are you being a wise steward of TIME? You will be held accountable at the Judgment Seat of Christ!

God reminds us that we are to redeem the time (Ephesians 5:16).

We must use our time to be a consistent example before the world.

Walk in wisdom
toward them that are without,
redeeming the time.

(Colossians 4:5)

✓ CHECKLIST FOR SPIRITUAL GROWTH

My Stewardship of Time

If "No" ... where do I stand spiritually, right now?

	YES	NO	Totally Lacking	Needs Improving
1. In my stewardship of Time ... am I giving God my "<u>precious</u>" time and not simply fitting in the Lord's work in my "spare" time?	☐	☐	☐	☐
2. In my time that I devote for my Lord ... is it "<u>quality</u>" time that I spend productively for His service?	☐	☐	☐	☐

(If you spend a great deal of time at your Church or in Christian activities which are primarily of a social nature ... young people's skiing weekends, bowling parties, recreation or fashion show ... this is not quality time for the Lord. You should check the "No" block.)

If you have checked the TOTALLY LACKING Box ... it means that, in this specific category ... spiritually ... you are failing. You need to realign your priorities ... and strive for spiritual growth, now!

If you checked NEEDS IMPROVEMENT Box ... it means that you are striving for a fulfilled Christian life ... but recognize your need to make further improvements.

As a believer, God's measure of blessing and answered prayer in your life will be directly proportionate to your full obedience to His Word.

8

OUR STEWARDSHIP OF TALENT

Talent is any natural ability in the learning or doing of anything.

* * *

That talent may be a gift that comes about without any special effort. It may come about because of our aptitude for a particular type of work. Much talent is acquired because of our interest or aptitude.

* * *

Christ does not judge our use of our talents by a worldly scale of popularity. This is not a Miss America contest!

* * *

You will recall that in the Scriptures (Luke 10:38-42), Mary's talent was one of simple devotion. Her sister, Martha, meanwhile, was busy exercising her talent of preparing dinner.

* * *

Don't downgrade yourself into believing you don't have any talents. Bathe your existing talents in dedicatory prayer, and seek additional talents that will be productive eternally.

8

OUR STEWARDSHIP OF TALENT

Everyone Has Talents

Too often when we think about talent, we assume it means someone who is a great singer, or a star athlete or one who plays a musical instrument well.

However, talent is any natural ability in the learning or doing of anything. That talent may be a gift that comes about without any special effort. It may come about because of our aptitude for a particular type of work. Much talent is acquired because of our interest or aptitude.

There may be one talent we excel in while we may also possess many other talents we can accomplish with relative ease.

God has enabled me to develop the talent of writing. This talent was not fully realized until I was 42 years of age. Within 10 years God used my talent to write some 30 books. My lesser talents include gardening, baking, making soups, and giving messages on Bible prophecy as well as teaching seminars on advertising techniques.

On the other hand, I have no talent for mathematics. I have no talent for playing a musical instrument. I was kicked out of violin class!

A Talent of Compassion

My wife, Mary, has talents I don't have. As I write this, she and 3 of her friends, Betty, Beryl and Genevieve have just come back from Inglis Home. This is a home for people with incurable diseases. Faithfully, each month these dedicated ladies arrive at the home, push wheelchair patients to the auditorium and present a gospel message. There is no fanfare, no earthly rewards. But they tithe this talent of compassion to reach the unloved for Christ!

Mary also has a talent

> *Distributing to the necessity of saints; given to hospitality.*
> (Romans 12:13)

In the last year we have entertained overnight:

A family of 10 people from Canada
Three missionary candidates
Four Bible school graduates en route to India
My sister and her family for one month (Their house had a devastating fire)
A retired missionary from China
A couple we met at Montrose Bible Conference
Two Pastors and their wives on two different occasions

And almost every Sunday, my wife prepares a Sunday dinner for anywhere from 5 to 20.

A Talent of Hospitality

Now this is not a talent of entertainment. It is a talent of hospitality, supporting others by prayer backed up with action! Each time, we have family devotions and all go away strengthened by the experience.

Christ does not judge our use of our talents by a worldly scale of popularity. This is not a Miss America contest.

You will recall that in the Scriptures (Luke 10:38–42), Mary's talent was one of simple devotion. She sat at the feet of Jesus, listening to Him attentively as He spoke.

Her sister Martha, meanwhile, was busy exercising her talent of preparing dinner.

Martha became annoyed at Mary's actions and asked the Lord if it was not un-
fair that she was doing all the work while
Mary was sitting at His feet.

Jesus reminder her of priorities in life and
in effect, said:

> Mary has discovered the one thing
> worth being concerned about . . .
> and I won't take it away from her.

**Talents
Used
Wisely**

We could travel down the personalities in
the Bible and discover that each of God's
children possessed certain talents. And
they used these talents wisely.

Person	Talent
Abraham	Faith
Daniel	Devotion
David	Ruling
Gideon	Valor
Moses	Leadership
Onesiphorus	Serving
Paul	Preaching
Timothy	Teaching
Abigail	Winsomeness
Deborah	Prophetess, Warrior
Esther	Dedication
Lydia	Hospitable
Ruth	Devotion
Vashti	Fearlessness

Don't downgrade yourself into believing
you don't have any talents. You do! You

The Christian Celebrity System

Several years ago, in an editorial in **Christian Herald,** Dr. Kenneth Wilson wrote the following.

I respect talent and I respect dedication.

But I am a little wary about exploiting either and especially about exploiting one against the other.

A great singer, who sings for God, is not doing God any particular favor. Must we constantly reassure ourselves, by featuring big-name testimonies, that God is for real? They won't take it on the say so of a garbage man . . . but let the word come from an astronaut . . . and WOW!

As things stand, the vocalist whose recording has sold a million copies makes a more promotable religious star than the quiet little lady in the church who may have lived much closer to the sharp edges of life's hurts and joys. He has a talent, and she hasn't . . . but a talent for what?

There were no celebrities when the faith began. A band of men had been challenged to be what they had never been . . . a challenge and a becoming that reached into every space and moment of their life.

Suppose they had done it our way. Take Peter, the big fisherman, for an example. After pondering on how to make his reputation work for Christ, they might have put out a press release:

This coming Pentecost,
Peter will preach!

Widely known as a former fisherman . . .
his record catch

when the weight almost sank the boat,
stands unbroken
in the Northern Galilee Fishing Conference!

Or this . . . about another of His disciples:

Matthew, notorious Tax Collector,
who last year
made a decision for Christ,
tells how he cheated for a living!

Hear the inside secrets
that will enable you
to save tax money!

I can't quite put my finger on it but there is something
that widely misses the mark when we make what was
and is . . . a dusty Galilean way of life . . . into a television special.

Maybe we should stop desperately hunting and using
celebrities. I am not sure that Jesus seeks first the big
man on campus . . . or what it proves when a Sunday
school teacher becomes Miss America!

may have a talent of holding the attention of children when teaching. It may be a talent of cooking, or baking. It may be a talent of listening! How many of us actually take time to listen to someone else! It may be a talent of counselling or comforting a troubled heart. It may be a talent of praying for missionaries worldwide. You may be a widow with a limited income. But each day, you faithfully pray for a select list of missionaries serving the Lord. You pray for unsaved loved ones. That dedicated talent is far greater in God's eyes than enjoying the popularity of the world.

Use Your Talents For the Lord

Seek those things you are best at doing whether it is making keys, tuning a car engine, baking a cake for a neighbor. Whatever your talents, exercise them as unto the Lord.

And, if you have no talent for preaching or teaching . . . all of us do have the talent of REACHING the lost. Each day hand someone a booklet or a book that will introduce that individual to Jesus Christ.

Bathe your existing talents in dedicatory prayer, and seek additional talents that will be productive eternally. The best use of our life is to spend it for something that will outlast it!

How wise a steward are you of your TALENTS? Remember, you will be held accountable at the Judgment Seat of Christ!

✓ CHECKLIST FOR SPIRITUAL GROWTH

My Stewardship of Talent

If "No" ... where do I stand spiritually, right now?

1. Do I have the Talent of Compassion and seek to reach out and help others without thought of any reward ... personally or financially?

   YES ☐   NO ☐   Totally Lacking ☐   Needs Improving ☐

2. With what little I have do I exercise the Talent of Hospitality without expecting it to be returned to me?

   YES ☐   NO ☐   Totally Lacking ☐   Needs Improving ☐

3. Do I faithfully pray for unsaved loved ones and for missionaries who are serving the Lord?

   YES ☐   NO ☐   Totally Lacking ☐   Needs Improving ☐

If you have checked the TOTALLY LACKING Box ... it means that, in this specific category ... spiritually ... you are failing. You need to realign your priorities ... and strive for spiritual growth, now!

If you checked NEEDS IMPROVEMENT Box ... it means that you are striving for a fulfilled Christian life ... but recognize your need to make further improvements.

As a believer, God's measure of blessing and answered prayer in your life will be directly proportionate to your full obedience to His Word.

JUDGMENTS and their DISTINCTION

1. Judgment of the Church *The Judgment Seat of Christ*
   (2 Corinthians 5:10-11)

Here we have the judgment of the believer's works ... not his sins. Hebrews 10:17 tells us that the Christian's sins and iniquities will be remembered no more. But Matthew 12:36, Romans 14:10, Colossians 3:24-25 remind us that every work must come to judgment. This judgment **occurs at the return of Christ for His church** (Rapture) ... immediately after the Rapture but before the marriage supper of the Lamb.

2. Judgment of individual Gentiles
   (Matthew 25:32)

This event is fully anticipated in the Old Testament. See Psalm 2:1-10, Isaiah 63:1-6, Joel 3:2-16; Zephaniah 3:8 and Zechariah 14:1-3.

Here the sheep (believers) are separated from the goats (unbelievers). This **occurs after the Tribulation Period** when those Gentiles who have come to Christ during this perilous period will be ushered into the kingdom and eternal life. The goats (unbelievers) will be cast into everlasting fire for their sins.

3. Judgment of Israel
   (Ezekiel 20:33-38)

When Christ returns **after the Tribulation Period** He will regather the Jews and purge those who rebelled. This will be accomplished after He first delivers the whole nation from its persecutors. Those who, like the sheep among the Gentiles, are believers in Jesus Christ will be ushered into the kingdom.

4. Judgment of the Wicked *The Great White Throne Judgment*
   (Revelation 20:11-15)

For this judgment we look to the time **after the Millennium** (1000 years). This last judgment comes to all unbelievers of all ages at the Great White Throne. The Holy God, the Sovereign Judge, will be seated on the throne. These unbelievers will be judged according to their sinful works. And because not one of them has his name written in the Lamb's book of life ... they will be cast into the lake of fire.

There will be no escape forever!

9

OUR STEWARDSHIP OF TREASURE

It is better to have your bank in Heaven than to have heaven in a bank!

* * *

There is a big difference between want and need. Food, shelter, clothing are basic **needs.** Yet, buying in excess in any of these categories can transform them into **wants.**

* * *

The money you earn is not yours because you earned it. It is yours, as a believer, because God has given you a holy trust.

* * *

You will be held accountable for your motives for giving to the Lord's work. Better for a poor widow to give $1 in love ... freely, than for a millionaire to give $1 Million with strings attached.

* * *

Possessions can become weights that hinder us in our spiritual progress. They may be the love of money, assets of silver, gold, costly jewels, stocks, bonds or family heirlooms.

* * *

The day will soon come when you will become accountable for your treasures at the Judgment Seat of Christ.

9

OUR STEWARDSHIP OF TREASURE

Poor Millionaires

A man whom others called poor, but who had just enough money to support himself, went about the country in the simplest way, studying and enjoying the life and beauty of it.

He once talked with a great millionaire who was engaged in business, working at it daily, and getting richer each week. The poor man said to the millionaire.

I am a richer man than you are.

The rich man look startled and asked:

How do you figure that?

The poor but contented man replied:

Why, I have as much money as I want, and you haven't!

How true this can be!

I know three millionaires. And they are always striving for *"One dollar more."*

From my personal observations, none of these three have found the real joys in life. One, in sorrow, confided to me that he could not afford to die because it would cost his estate too much money.

It was Lincoln who had no great admiration for mere financial success. He once said:

> *Financial success is purely metallic. The man who gains it has four metallic attributes:*
>
> **Gold** *in his palm*
> **Silver** *on his tongue*
> **Brass** *in his face*
> **Iron** *in his heart.*

Oswald J. Smith, the former Pastor of People's Church in Toronto has said:

> *I have learned that money*
>   *is not the measure of a man,*
> *but it is often the means of*
>   *finding out how small he is.*

The Right Bank

It is better to have your bank in Heaven than to have your heaven in a bank.

Not only often will a man rob God, but he will take an income tax deduction on it.

Many people have the mistaken impression that the percentage of their income they give to the Lord each week should be figured on their net income after taxes. In my opinion, this is wrong!

Let's suppose your income before taxes is $300 a week and you have decided to give God 10%. That 10% should be based on the $300 or $30. It should not be based on the net income after the Government has taken out their taxes. If the Government taxes your GROSS total income . . . should not God's share also be based on your total (before taxed) income? Of course!

How many believers are spending most of their time in the pursuit of earning more money . . . husbands holding down two jobs, mothers working! We justify this by saying that the cost of living has risen and it takes all this effort just to make ends meet.

Needs vs. Wants

In many cases, the basic problem is not just making ends meet but rather living beyond our needs. There is a big difference between want and need.

How To Solve Financial Problems

Most families, unless they have inherited wealth, find it increasingly difficult to meet all their financial obligations. It has not been unusual for churches to go into bankruptcy. As we enter the Last Days, the spiral of inflation will make these problems accelerate. Here are some guidelines that will help you solve these difficulties, Scripturally!

1. **Eliminate idols in your life.** They will separate you from God. Are what you consider necessities really luxuries? Write down how you spend your time each week and where your money goes. Faithfully cut out those things that would divert you from God.

2. **Make sure you first return to God the first fruits of your labor.** Anything over 1/10th is an offering.

Food, shelter, clothing are basic **needs.** Yet they can become **wants.** Here are some examples of wants . . . not needs.

1. **Food**

   Spending money unwisely for hollow foods that tear down our body. Eating out frequently as opposed to eating a nourishing, economical home-cooked meal. Overeating.

2. **Shelter**

   Spending money on a luxurious home far beyond our basic necessity. Putting in a swimming pool, a tennis court or other non-essentials.

3. **Clothing**

   Becoming obsessed with keeping in style each season. Have you ever had the responsibility of going through the belongings of a relative who had a stroke or died and discovered boxes of shoe laces, batteries, suits, shoes, radios, shirts and ties . . . all new and never opened? I have! This is another example of owning a large array of dresses or suits, or shoes far beyond practicality.

If you are honest, it will be easy for you to determine the line between needs and wants in your life and the lives of those in your family.

Things That Weigh Us Down

If your home and your life is alrady filled with a great many fulfilled wants . . . then it is time to reassess our direction in life. It is time to dispense with these weights which can easily destroy our testimony and our eternal rewards.

For we will be held accountable not only as to how much money we give to the Lord's work . . . but also, how wisely we administered the money to which God entrusted us.

The money you earn is not yours because you earned it. It is yours, as a believer, because God has given you a holy trust.

It would be wise for you to read carefully Matthew 25:14-30. This is the parable of the Talents.

A Talent was a weight of silver or gold of extremely high value. Jesus Christ told this parable to emphasize the need for faithful service until His coming again at the Rapture.

The man who was going into a far country actually refers to Christ and His ascension after His crucifixion.

Money will buy
a bed but not sleep
books but not brains
food but not appetite
finery but not beauty
medicine but not health
amusement but not happiness
a Bible but not eternal life!

**A Day
of
Accounting**

In the parable the man gives $5000 to one servant, $2000 to another and $1000 to the last . . . dividing the money according to their abilities.

> The first two servants
>   doubled their money.
> The third servant was not challenged
>   by this opportunity and therefore
>   displayed no diligence. He simply
>   hid his money in the ground.

When the Master returned He called on each one to give an account as to how well they administered the money given to them in trust. To the first two servants who were wise stewards of the Lord's money, He said:

> *Well done, good and faithful servant;*
> *thou hast been faithful over a few things,*
> *I will make thee ruler over many things:*
> *Enter thou*
>   *into the joy of thy Lord.*
>   (Matthew 25:21,23)

The third servant, because of his selfish neglect, lost out on the joy of God's blessings. When the accounting day came, he was found wanting!

**Accountable
For Our
Motives**

Weekly income is not the only form of money for which we will be held accountable.

We will also be held accountable for our motives for giving to the Lord's work. I know of several people who have given large amounts of money, if the building would be named in their honor or in the honor of someone in their family. Better for a poor widow to give $1 in love . . . freely than for a millionaire to give $1 Million with strings attached. God sees the heart!

You may not realize that you will also be held accountable for those things you have accumulated in the past. They may be items or things that you paid good money for and such an expenditure was a want . . . not a need . . . which robbed God of what should be His!

It may be a sterling silver set. A close relative of mine cashed in his sterling silver and used the proceeds for basic necessities. When asked why he disposed of this family heirloom, he commented:

Steak tastes just as good
off of stainless steel.

Accountable For Our Possessions

How true! How many china closets display silver bowls, silver sets, or expensive china! This money could be used for the Lord in the winning of souls to Christ worldwide. It is another way Satan siphons off our financial trust so it doesn't reach mission fields.

Self-righteously, we may say . . . *But, last year we gave 10% of our income to missions.* That's good, but was it best? Doesn't our Lord deserve the very best and the most?

Perhaps we have a large collection of stamps, of coins, or commemorative plates. Perhaps you own Treasury Bonds, stocks and bonds, diamonds, gold or costly jewelry, and you never want to part with them.

There are no pockets in a shroud!

Now is the time to put your Talents . . . your financial assets . . . to work for the Lord . . . doubling or tripling that to which He has entrusted in your care!

One day . . . and it could be very soon . . . perhaps even tomorrow . . . the Master will return. He will call your name to step forward for an accounting.

**No
Second
Chance**

At that point you will suddenly realize how foolish you were in carefully guarding and hoarding that silverware, that costly jewelry, that safe deposit box of stocks and bonds all for your own personal gain and pride.

But then it will be too late!

Your rewards will be lost!

There will not be a second chance!

**The
Burden
Of
Possessions**

Alexander the Great was marching on Persia. It looked as if the great empire was about to crumble, as later it did, before his armies.

There was a critical moment, however, which nearly resulted in disaster.

The army has taken spoils of silver, gold and other treasures in such quantities that the soldiers were literally weighed down with them.

Discovering The Secret Of Being CONTENT!

Listen to Our Lord as He reminds us:

Godliness with contentment is great gain.

For we brought nothing
*   into this world,*
and it is certain
*   we can carry nothing out.*

And having food and raiment
*   let us be therewith content.*

They that will be rich
*   fall into temptation and a snare*
*   and into many foolish and hurtful lusts,*
*   which drown men*
*   in destruction and perdition.*

For the love of money
*   is the root of all evil:*
Which, while some coveted after,
*   they have erred from the faith,*
*   and pierced themselves through*
*   with many sorrows.*

(1 Timothy 6:6-10)

The apostle Paul had many problems! Life was a great deal easier for him when he was a simple tentmaker in his hometown of Tarsus.

It should be evident to us from Paul's own life in Christ, that **success (from a worldly viewpoint) is not a measure of God's blessing on a ministry!**

After he met God and dedicated his life to serving Him, he recalls in 2 Corinthians 11:24-27: **(1)** Five times he received 39 lashes **(2)** Three times he was beaten with rods **(3)** Once he was stoned **(4)** Three times he was shipwrecked and **(5)** Often he was without food and water. Yet, Paul reminds us in Philippians 4:11 . . . that regardless of circumstances . . . we should be **content!**

Alexander gathered all the treasures together in one great pile and set fire to them.

The soldiers were furious. But it was not long before they realized the wisdom of their leader.

It was as if wings had been given to them—they walked lightly again, unfettered by extra weight. The campaign proceeded to victory.

Weights That Hinder

Examine closely those weights that hinder our ministry to the Lord. They may be the love of money, hidden assets of silver, gold, costly jewels, stocks, bonds or family heirlooms.

Then determine to turn your silver into souls. Don't let Satan siphon that which is the Lord's and rob you of your eternal rewards. For the day will soon come when you will become accountable for your treasures at the Judgment Seat of Christ.

God's Word reminds us:

The sleep of a laboring man is sweet,
whether he eat little or much:
but the abundance of the rich
will not suffer him to sleep.

There is a grievous evil . . .
riches being hoarded by their owner
to his hurt . . .

Ecclesiastes 5:12,13

HOW MUCH WILL IT COST?

We are living in a day and age when people are concerned about costs.

Many wealthy businessmen in New York, fed up with the high-paced living of the city, have given up their entire business or occupation simply to be able to move out into the country and get back to basic living. While in the entire United States there are only 55 people per square mile ... the density of population in Manhattan is 25,000 people per square mile! And with more people, come more services and more costs. So critical is the problem that New York City is seriously thinking about separating itself from New York State and become an independent state of itself. The reason ... a desperate need for money.

Everywhere one turns costs have risen at a faster proportion than income. Already 1 out of every 3 people in the United States receive some type of Federal or state aid. And along with Federal taxes, many are paying not only state and sales taxes but also city taxes.

It becomes too expensive to become ill and enter a hospital. Hospital rooms which once were $20 a day some 10 or 15 years ago have now zoomed to over $150 a day. It is predicted that in 10 more years or less they will be $500 a day.

Housewives are concerned about rising food costs. Can you remember when milk was 15¢ or 20¢ a quart and when a loaf of bread was 5¢? The penny stamp and penny candy have long been phased out.

We have been caught up in the convenience items of the world. And with the rise in our standard of living ... comes a greater struggle just to maintain some sensible balance ... not only of our budget, but of our testimony.

Too often when we are pressed on every side there is a human tendency to deny Christ to meet our material desires.

How important it is to look into our life to see if we are conforming to this world. Paul in Romans 12:2 reminds us to". . . be not conformed to this world: but be ye transformed. . . . "

And this transformation may demand a far greater cost than any earthly cost.

How much does it cost to live as a Christian? It may cost us some friends. It may cost us that extra car. It may cost us that second home. It may cost us those added luxuries. It may cost us some time we normally would spend at the seashore or mountains. It may cost us an evening of bowling or fishing. **It may even cost us our life!**

To the Christian who is really dedicated to Christ . . . will come tribulation . . . but we know that He (Christ) has overcome the world and our present trial worketh for but a season.

The price one pays for being a Christian will result in a Crown of Glory. But the price one pays for denying Christ will be an eternity in hell.

How much does it cost?

It cost Jesus Christ His life!

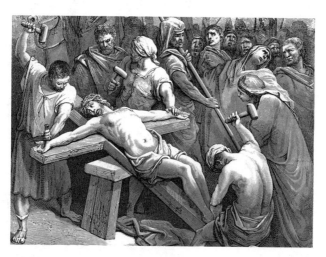

Wherefore,
seeing we also are compassed about
  with so great a cloud of witnesses,
let us
  lay aside every weight,
  and the sin
  which doth so easily beset us,
and let us
  run with patience
  the race
  that is set before us.

Looking unto Jesus,
  the author
  and finisher
  of our faith,
Who for the joy
  that was set before Him
  endured the cross,
  despising the shame,
  and is set down at the right hand
  of the throne of God.
                    (Hebrews 12:1,2)

How can I do less
Than give Him my best
  And live for Him completely . . .
After all
He has done for me!

✓CHECKLIST FOR SPIRITUAL GROWTH

My Stewardship of Treasure

If "No" ... where do I stand spiritually, right now?

		Totally Lacking	Needs Improving
1. Does my daily life and actions reflect that I am more interested in the Bank of Heaven than to have heaven in my earthly bank?	YES ☐ NO ☐	☐	☐
2. Have I learned to wisely determine the difference between <u>needs</u> and <u>wants</u> and does my spending reflect proper use of the Lord's money?	YES ☐ NO ☐	☐	☐
3. Have I successfully rid myself of weights that hinder my ministry to the Lord?	YES ☐ NO ☐	☐	☐

(If your home is filled with needless, seldom used possessions, and you own stocks, bonds, diamonds, gold where God has not been given <u>at least</u> one-tenth of <u>their</u> value ... then these possessions are weights that hinder. You should check the "No" block.)

If you have checked the TOTALLY LACKING Box ... it means that, in this specific category ... spiritually ... you are failing. You need to realign your priorities ... and strive for spiritual growth, now!

If you checked NEEDS IMPROVEMENT Box ... it means that you are striving for a fulfilled Christian life ... but recognize your need to make further improvements.

As a believer, God's measure of blessing and answered prayer in your life will be directly proportionate to your full obedience to His Word.

JUDGMENT DAYS

JUDGMENT OF UNBELIEVERS

BOOK OF LIFE

THE BOOKS OPENED

"And whosoever was not found written in the book of life was cast into the Lake of Fire." (Rev. 20:15)

LAKE OF FIRE

". . . the tares are the children of the wicked one. The enemy that sowed them is the devil; the harvest is the end of the world; and the reapers are the angels. As therefore the tares are gathered and burned in the fire; so shall it be in the end of this world" (Matthew 13: 38-40)

1000 YEAR MILLENNIUM

REWARD JUDGMENTS FOR BELIEVERS

"and I will dwell in the house of the Lord for ever." (Psalm 23:6)

INCORRUPTIBLE CROWN (Victor's Crown)
". . . every man that striveth for the mastery is temperate in all things . . . they do it to obtain a corruptible crown; we an INCORRUPTIBLE." (I Corinthians 9:25)

CROWN OF REJOICING (Soul Winner's Crown)
". . . what is our hope . . . or crown of rejoicing? Are not even ye in the presence of our Lord Jesus Christ at His coming? For ye are our glory and joy." (I Thessalonians 2:19, 20)

CROWN OF RIGHTEOUSNESS
"Henceforth there is laid up for me a crown of righteousness, which the Lord, the righteous judge, shall give me at that day: and not to me only, but unto all them also that love His appearing." (II Timothy 4:8)

CROWN OF GLORY (Crown for Service)
"Feed the flock of God which is among you . . . (be) examples to the flock . . . And when the chief Shepherd shall appear, ye shall receive a crown of glory that fadeth not away." (I Peter 5:2-4)

CROWN OF LIFE (Martyr's Crown)
". . . the devil shall cast some of you into prison, that ye may be tried . . . be thou faithful unto death, and I will give thee a crown of life." (Revelation 2:10)

"Every man's work shall be made manifest . . . because it shall be revealed by fire . . . if any man's work abide . . . he shall receive a reward . . . if any man's work shall be burned, he shall suffer loss: but he himself shall be saved; yet so as by fire." (I Corinthians 3:13-15)

WOOD
HAY
STUBBLE

GOLD | PRECIOUS STONES

SILVER

RAPTURE
BELIEVERS meet CHRIST in the air

10

OUR WILLINGNESS

A willingness is a desire to do something readily, gladly and voluntarily!

* * *

To know God's will is man's greatest treasure. To do His will is life's greatest privilege.

* * *

<u>Outside</u> of the will of God there is no such thing as success. <u>In</u> the will of God, there cannot be any failure!

* * *

At the Judgment Seat of Christ, you will be judged on your willingness, obedience, and service while on earth.

* * *

If you were to take an accounting today, how would you stand? Are improvements needed in your walk with God? If we are faithful in our accountability to God, we can look forward to a glorious triumph sharing in treasured trophies!

10

OUR WILLINGNESS

Readily And Gladly

A willingness is a desire to do something readily, gladly and voluntarily.

As a child, do you remember when your mother or dad asked you to do something. Perhaps it was a request to put out the trash on trash day or clean your room.

You should have done it readily . . . immediately upon request. But you had to be reminded. You thought it was nagging . . . those constant reminders.

With a displeased look on your face, and after repeated requests to put out the trash, you finally did so . . . but not gladly.

You waited until you were told. You never did bother to figure out how the trash would be disposed of. It could overflow the sink and the wastebaskets and still you probably would hope it would go out by itself. Voluntarily you should have seen the need and accomplished this task on your own free will, readily and gladly. That you finally did put out the trash earned no praise nor commendation, for it was not done with a willing heart!

Perhaps you received an allowance weekly for accomplishing certain duties in the house. Even though you did ac-

complish these responsibilities faithfully
... the money allowance was the incen-
tive. Nevertheless, the work should have
been done with a willing heart. Was it?

At the Judgment Seat of Christ we will be
held accountable for our willingness. Did
we serve the Lord with a willing heart or
did we serve Him because of fear or for
favor.

How thankful we can be that God was willing, readily, gladly and voluntarily to free
man from his sin and eternal damnation.

The Lord is not slack
  concerning His promise . . .
but is long-suffering to us-ward,
  not willing
    that any should perish,
but that all should come to repentence.
                              (2 Peter 3:9)

God's son, Jesus Christ was also willing.

. . . Lo, I come to do Thy will, O God.
                              (Hebrews 10:9)

**Christ
Was
Willing**

In saying the above, Christ had to be willing even to accept crucifixion if it were so
demanded of Him by the Father. And you
will recall at Gethsemane, Jesus prayed
asking God if this hour of testing might
pass for Him. Yet He was willing:

. . . Abba, Father,
all things are possible unto thee;
take away this cup from Me:
  nevertheless not what I will,
but what Thou wilt.
                              (Mark 14:36)

Too often the concept is conveyed by some evangelists and ministers that, in following Christ, we will have a life of only abundance and happiness. This is contrary to Scripture.

God reveals to us:

> . . . all that will live godly
>   in Christ Jesus
> shall suffer persecution.
>
> (2 Timothy 3:12)

> Thou therefore endure hardness,
> as a good soldier of Jesus Christ.
>
> (2 Timothy 2:3)

We are also reminded that life should be directed heavenward:

> No man that warreth
> entangleth himself
>   with the affairs of this life.
>
> (2 Timothy 2:4)

Don't Give Up!

Therefore, there has to be a willingness to triumph through trials. And I admit, this can be difficult at times. There have been times in my life when I just felt like giving up! I had expected slings and arrows from those who were **not** Christians.

But there have been times when such testings come from those who called themselves my fellow believers. Their lack of love, their lack of understanding, their lack of compassion has several times brought me to the brink of calling it quits. In pity, I would ask myself: "Why should I knock myself out writing and publishing books to win souls to Christ. The aggravation simply isn't worth it!"

**We
Shall
Reap**

Then, after speaking in a church, a widow woman would come up to me and with tears in her eyes, would relate how her husband accepted Christ after reading one of my books. And then she would add, something like this:

Odd! John never did read books and he would seldom come to church. But God used your books to reach his heart.

That's why I determined . . . from my very first book to have as the last chapter of each book a Decision Chapter pointing the reader to Christ.

Suddenly . . . all the aggravation, all the trials seemed to vanish.

I realized that I must be willing to deny myself. I must be willing to endure hardness as a good soldier of Jesus Christ. I must be willing to be willing!

**Willing
To Be
Willing**

Willing to be willing! That's the key! That willingness should be fired from the fact of the grace of the Lord Jesus Christ that:

*. . . though He was rich,
yet for your sakes
   He became poor,
that ye
   through His poverty
might be rich!*   (2 Corinthians 8:9)

In light of this we are told:

*Now therefore
perform the doing of it;
that as there was a readiness to will,
so there may be a performance . . .*
          (2 Corinthians 8:11)

**Follow
Through**

You may recall the parable of the two sons in Matthew 21:28-32. The older boy was told to go out and work on the farm that day. The boy refused, but later he changed his mind and went to work on the farm.

The father then told the younger boy to go work on the farm. The younger boy said he would . . . but he didn't!

When Jesus asked the chief priests which of the two was obeying his father, they replied that the older boy was the one who obeyed.

Jesus was conveying to the Sanhedrins that the outcasts, such as publicans and harlots, who eventually accepted Christ's message became followers of Jesus (Luke 15:1,2). They had at first refused . . . but then accepted.

But the son who said he would go, but did not, was like the pharisaical religious leaders who gave an aloof assent to following God but never really followed through. See John 5:35 and Luke 7:29,30.

How willing are you?

To know God's will, is man's greatest treasure...
To do His will, is life's greatest privilege!

Don't
Make
Excuses

When God confronted Moses at the burning bush, He commissioned Moses to lead His people to the Promised Land.

Moses was not at first willing to accept the heavy responsibility of such leadership. He made several excuses.

A. The people will not believe me.
B. They won't do what I tell them.
C. I am not a good speaker.
D. I am slow of speech and have an awkward tongue.

Then Moses topped all of this off with his final excuse which, in effect, said:

Lord, here am I, send Aaron!

It is a good thing to be humble. But it is a bad thing to be unwilling when God calls.

Our unwillingness is housed in many excuses. To us they may appear valid.

I cannot go to the mission field . . .
  because my mother is sick . . .
  because I do not feel called . . .
  God has not given me a definite sign . . .

The mission I applied to
  turned me down . . .
I'm too old . . .
I'm too young
  there are things I want to do first.

All these may appear to be valid excuses in the above example dealing with one phase of Christian dedication.

But they parallel the same type of unwillingness shown by Moses some 3300 years ago!

Jesus charges the deaf and dumb spirits to come out of the boy and challenges the father to believe! See Mark 9:23. Our unbelief is the greatest hindrance in our way towards spiritual victory!

**God
Will
Provide**

Our unwillingness is countered by God's willingnesses. In Exodus 3:1-21, he affirms to Moses:

A. I will send thee   (v. 10)
B. I will be with thee   (v. 12)
C. I will bring you out   (v. 17)
D. I will stretch forth My hand (v. 20)
E. I will give this people favor (v. 21)

The response of Moses was somewhat like the response of the father who approached Jesus bringing his son who was in convulsions with demons.

The father pleaded with Jesus to cast out this demon . . . *if thou canst do any thing . . .*" (Mark 9:22).

Jesus confronted him and said:

*If thou canst believe,
all things are possible
to him that believeth.*

(Mark 9:23)

The father, with tears in his eyes, cried out:

*Lord,
I believe;
Help thou
my unbelief!*

(Mark 9:24)

Moses believed God, but his unwilling spirit diluted his faith into what appeared to be unbelief!

**Let Go
And
Let God**

Anguish must have filled the father's heart as he watched his son suffering in demon possession, writhing on the ground. The father did believe Jesus. Yet he was unable to commit that belief wholly by faith. He was struggling with an unbelief that was robbing his entire life of abiding joy in Jesus.

His belief was good. Yet he had to escalate his faith to better and finally to BEST.

Two seemingly contradictory terms . . . belief . . . unbelief! Does that portray your life in Christ?

Do you believe Christ is able, really able to meet every need? Yet, in actual daily life, do your actions convey unbelief?

Are you willing . . . really willing to do the Lord's will each and every day. Are you willing . . . really willing to abide within the shelter of His arms through every circumstance?

If not, are you willing to be made willing? Psalm 110:3 speaks of a willing spirit. Matthew 26:41 reveals a willing spirit but a flesh that is not willing. This is when Christ found His disciples asleep in Gethsemane and He commanded.

**A
Willing
Spirit**

*Watch and pray,
    that ye enter not into temptation:
the spirit indeed is willing,
but the flesh is weak.*

To know God's will is man's greatest treasure. To do His will is life's greatest privilege!

**Wise
Advice**

My daughter, Diane, has reminded me of several verses that challenge us to become willing. One of them is David's advice to his son, Solomon:

> . . . know thou the God of thy father,
> and serve Him with a perfect heart
>   and with a willing mind:
> for the Lord searcheth all hearts,
> and understands every intent of the
>   thoughts:
> if thou seek Him,
>   He will be found of thee;
> but if thou forsake Him,
>   He will cast thee off for ever.
>   (1 Chronicles 28:9)

Outside of the will of God there is no such thing as success. In the will of God, there cannot be any failure.

God has given us a will with which to choose His will. Too often our life is self-centered instead of God-centered. It reminds me of a tea party.

> I had a little tea party
> This afternoon at three,
>   'Twas very small—
>   Three guests in all—
>   Just I, Myself and Me.
>
> Myself ate all the sandwiches
> While I drank up the tea;
> 'Twas also I who ate the pie
>   And passed the cake to me!

Would you like God's best for your life? Then you must be willing to follow His command. If, right now, you are not willing . . . are you willing to be willing?

A Final Judgment

At the Judgment Seat of Christ, you will be judged on your willingness, obedience, and service while on earth.

> EVERY ONE OF US SHALL GIVE AN ACCOUNT OF HIMSELF TO GOD!
>
> ROMANS 14: 12

That accounting will include:

A. Our attitude towards God
B. Our attitude towards others
C. Our prayer life
D. Our priorities
E. Our motives
F. Our stewardship of
   1. Talents
   2. Time
   3. Treasure
G. Our willingness

If you were to take that accounting today, how would you stand? Are improvements needed in your walk with God? If so, should you not begin to make those improvements right now . . . starting today?

**Precious
Promise**

Roy E. Pulliam, 22 years a faithful teacher at Prairie Bible Institute in Three Hills, Alberta, Canada, revealed the precious promise of Psalm 126:6.

Its truth is divided into 5 **"T's"**.

> *He that goeth forth:* **Toil**
> *and weepeth:* **Tears**
> *bearing precious seed:* **Treasure**
> *shall doubtless come again*
>   *with rejoicing:* **Triumph**
> *bringing his sheaves with him:*
> **Trophies**

What a precious promise this is for every believer! If we are faithful in our accountability to God, we can look forward to a glorious triumph sharing in treasured trophies!

> *Lay not up for yourselves*
>   *treasures upon earth,*
>   *where moth and rust doth corrupt,*
> *and where thieves*
>   *break through and steal:*
> *But lay up for yourselves*
>   *treasures in Heaven,*
>   *where neither moth nor rust doth*
>   *corrupt,*
>   *and where thieves*
>   *do not break through nor steal:*
> *For where your treasure is,*
> *there will your heart be also.*
>
> (Matthew 6:19–21)

Is our all-consuming fire
        To lay up treasures for
                our desire,
        To voice Christ's name
                for public show
But serve ourself on
                earth below?
Or do we really seek His face
        To serve Him through
                life's daily race,
        To make our joy in
                Him complete
To cast our Crowns
                at Jesus' feet!

**Seek
Those Things
Above**

Only you can answer that question. Honestly, search your life, your motives. And ask the Holy Spirit to:

> *Search me, O God,*
> *and know my heart:*
> *Try me,*
> *and know my thoughts:*
> *And see if there be*
> *any wicked way in me,*
> *And lead me in the way everlasting.*
> (Psalm 139:23, 24)

You will, as a believer, be held accountable at the Judgment Seat of Christ. Your salvation is not in question at this Judgment Seat. Yet this accountability will determine what rewards, if any, will be yours eternally!

In light of this:

> *Seek those things which are above*
> *. . .*
> *Set your affection (your mind)*
> *on things above,*
> *not on things on the earth.*
> *. . . and* **all** *these things*
> *shall be added unto you.*
> (Colossians 3:1, 2; Matthew 6:33)

✓ CHECKLIST FOR SPIRITUAL GROWTH

My Willingness

If "No" ... where do I stand spiritually, right now?

			Totally Lacking	Needs Improving

1. When God gives direction in your life, do you follow this calling willingly?
   YES ☐ | NO ☐ | Totally Lacking ☐ | Needs Improving ☐

2. If God should call you to give up your present job and serve Him on the mission field ... would you do so willingly?
   YES ☐ | NO ☐ | Totally Lacking ☐ | Needs Improving ☐

3. If God should call you to sell your present home and move into a smaller home, getting rid of material possessions you don't really need ... would you be willing to do so?
   YES ☐ | NO ☐ | Totally Lacking ☐ | Needs Improving ☐

4. If God should call you to convert into cash your assets in stocks, bonds, silver, gold and diamonds and give this cash to soul winning missionary ministries for God ... would you do so willingly?
   YES ☐ | NO ☐ | Totally Lacking ☐ | Needs Improving ☐

5. If you have answered "No" to any of the above four questions ... then, would you be willing to be made willing?
   YES ☐ | NO ☐ | Totally Lacking ☐ | Needs Improving ☐

If you have checked the TOTALLY LACKING Box ... it means that, in this specific category ... spiritually ... you are failing. You need to realign your priorities ... and strive for spiritual growth, now!

If you checked NEEDS IMPROVEMENT Box ... it means that you are striving for a fulfilled Christian life ... but recognize your need to make further improvements.

As a believer, God's measure of blessing and answered prayer in your life will be directly proportionate to your full obedience to His Word.

Use this ORDER FORM to order additional copies of

HOW TO BE SURE OF CROWNS IN HEAVEN
by Salem Kirban

You will want to give **HOW TO BE SURE OF CROWNS IN HEAVEN** to your loved ones and friends.

An excellent book to give to those who want to know how to prepare for their future according to guidelines set forth in God's Word. This book can become a gift with eternal values!

PRICES

1 copy: $4.95

3 copies: $12 (You save $2.85)
5 copies: $20 (You save $4.74)

ORDER FORM

Salem Kirban, Inc.
Kent Road
Huntingdon Valley, Pennsylvania 19006

Enclosed find $_____ for _____ copies of
HOW TO BE SURE OF CROWNS IN HEAVEN
by Salem Kirban
*I will pay UPS for small delivery charge.

Name_____
    Mr./Mrs./Miss   (Please PRINT)

Street_____

City_____

State_____Zip Code_____

*If your local Christian bookstore cannot supply you . . . you may order direct. To insure safe arrival, books will be shipped via United Parcel Service. **(1)** You will pay UPS for small delivery charge. **(2)** For actual cost of books, send check direct to:
SALEM KIRBAN, Inc., 2117 Kent Rd., Huntingdon Valley, Pa. 19006 U.S.A.

A NEW STANDARD of EXCELLENCE!

10 REASONS WHY!
On the other side are 10 reasons why we believe this is the first *really* new Bible since the 1909 Scofield Reference Bible!

"I have reviewed Salem Kirban's REFERENCE BIBLE and find it to be a source of real inspiration. Salem Kirban has excited our nation with his many prophetical releases and brought men to a realization of the fact that Jesus Christ's coming is at hand. I believe Salem Kirban's many works on prophecy have created a longing in the hearts of believers to see Jesus . . ."
DR. JACK VAN IMPE

"I've already taken the REFERENCE BIBLE to church with me, and became so fascinated that I almost missed Jack Hayford's sermon. I think it's wonderful to have the King James Bible itself, along with the rich benefits of Salem Kirban's own intense and extensive study. There's just so much! It's a very valuable combination . . . and I'm delighted to have it persondlly."
PAT BOONE

The Salem Kirban
REFERENCE BIBLE

NOW! AT LAST! A BIBLE WITH 2000 PAGES OF HELPS TO MEET EVERY NEED IN YOUR LIFE!

Salem Kirban's
REFERENCE BIBLE
KING JAMES VERSION

Now, the world's best **seller** will become the best **read** in your home! Salem Kirban has taken the beloved King James Version and added 2000 pages of crystal-clear Commentary. Here are 10 reasons why many acclaim that this Bible is the first really new Bible since the 1909 Scofield. Over 500 photos and charts **Full Color.** Only 1¾" thick. Handy to carry to church!

10 EXCLUSIVE Features NO OTHER BIBLE HAS!

1. Commentary on Every Page Unlocks Guidelines for Living

Salem Kirban
In his clear, descriptive style, Salem Kirban's Commentary Notes appear on **over** 1000 of the Bible text pages. He is the author of over 35 books!

Gary G. Cohen
Dr. Cohen clearly explains the 100 most difficult Bible passages. Dr. Cohen is Executive Vice President of Clearwater Christian College.

Charles Haddon Spurgeon
The most famous preacher of the 19th century. His devotional Commentary *(written during his greatest trials)* are on over 300 pages.

2. Promise Verses In Margin

When you need faith and courage . . . often the Promise Verses in the Bible are hard to find because these gems lie buried in the text. We have highlighted these Promise Verses in yellow (in the text) and **also** repeated the same verse in the MARGIN of the same page. Now, by leafing through your Bible, you can each day

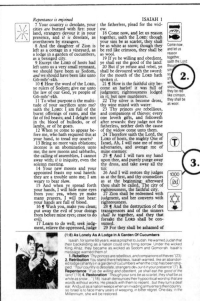

Sample Page — Actual Page Size: 6" x 9"

select a Promise To Live By! See sample page in this column.

3. Time Period Symbols

The Bible is confusing to many because they do not realize that the text refers to 3 basic Time Periods (past, present and future). Within these 3 Time Periods are at least 15 **further** Time Divisions! In the margin of each page of The Salem Kirban REFERENCE BIBLE, the Time Symbol Picture helps you identify the correct Time Period . . . making God's promises so much richer to you and to your loved ones

Scattering of Israel

Current World

Continual Promise

Rapture

Armageddon

Judgment Seat of Christ

Marriage of the Lamb

Judgment of Nation Israel

4. Rare, Old Bible Etchings

Unusual etchings of Bible scenes designed by craftsmen over 100 years ago. Enjoy the same etchings your great grandparents found joy and comfort in!

5. Full Color Holy Land Photographs

Vivid photographs taken by Salem Kirban reveal the beauty of the Promised Land as it is **right now** . . . today!

6. Full Color Charts on Future Events

Over 50 Charts including the 21 Tribulation Judgments, Three Coming Decisive Wars, The Three Heavens, The Resurrections. A few are picture below in reduced size.

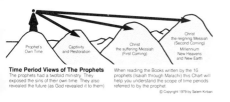

Time Period Views of The Prophets
The prophets had a twofold ministry. They exposed the sins of their own time. They also revealed the future (as God revealed it to them)

When reading the Books written by the 16 prophets (Isaiah through Malachi) this Chart will help you understand the scope of time periods referred to by the prophet

© Copyright 1979 by Salem Kirban

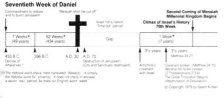

© Copyright 1979 by Salem Kirban

7. 380 Page Commentary on The Book of REVELATION

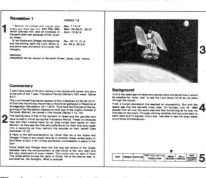

The last book in the Bible, **Revelation,** deals with future events and is the most difficult book for many to understand. We have Visualized the book by **1** placing only 2 verses on each page **2** writing a clear Commentary **3** including an explanatory illustration **4** tying the verses in to current events and **5** by a red arrow, pointing to the proper Time Period!

8. Major Doctrines Explained

There are at least 28 major Doctrines in the Bible. These DOCTRINES are explained in Commentary units marked with this Symbol placed next to identifying verse!

9. Major Attributes Explained

There are 17 Attributes (or characteristics) that identify God! Each ATTRIBUTE is explained in Commentary units marked with this Symbol placed next to identifying verse!

10. Extra NEW TESTAMENT Commentary

As an added bonus, you will discover **100 added pages** of special New Testament Commentary. All in FULL COLOR. Includes many Charts, Maps and Graphs!

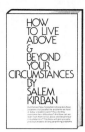

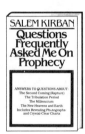

Salem Kirban
DOCTRINES OF DECEPTION Series

Salem Kirban devoted a year studying each one of the 4 major cults. As an investigative reporter he visited headquarters and researched the origins of each cult. He carefully studied the background of each founder to search out the reasons the cult was started.

You will find these books *highly interesting* and very easy-to-read. Salem Kirban traces the adventurous beginnings of each cult on up to the present day. Includes rare photographs. **EXCLUSIVE FEATURE.** Each individual cult book has a **Cult Decoder.** This unique chart quickly shows at a glance how the cult departs from Scripture.

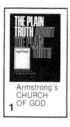

Armstrong's CHURCH OF GOD
1

JEHOVAH'S WITNESSES
2

MORMONISM
3

CHRISTIAN SCIENCE
4

1 Armstrong's Church of God (The Plain Truth)

Why is Herbert W. Armstrong's cult considered the most deceptive of all cults? Why do even Christians fall into the snare set by the Armstrong trap? Why is *The Plain Truth* simply not the Plain Truth? What importance did the "neighbor next door" have to do with this strange cult? What is the secret of Armstrong's growth? How is the operation financed? How does it win and hold converts? What promises does it take from Israel?

2 Jehovah's Witnesses

How is it possible for this group to print 50,000 books a day in their Brooklyn Headquarters? How has the Watchtower magazine catapulted Jehovah's Witnesses into the fastest growing cult today? Why did Mrs. Russell ask for a divorce? Why did Judge Rutherford go to jail? What is each member of their congregation required to do? Who are their 144,000? Why is the date 1914 so important to them?

3 Mormonism

Who are those young men with that well-scrubbed look who knock on doors? Why do they do it? Why do they pay their own way as Mormon missionaries? What strange findings that first began with eight barges and an ocean trip gave birth to an unusual cult? Why did they build a $2 million vault in the Granite Mountains near Salt Lake City? What state in the United States will possess the "keys to the world power?"

4 Christian Science

Why do Christian Scientists owe their origin to a horse? Who was Phineas Quimby and why do Christian Scientists hate to hear his name mentioned? What tragedies occurred in Mary Baker Eddy's life that triggered her search for a new religion? Why did Dr. Noyes remove Mary Baker Eddy's husband's heart and show it to her in her own living room? How vast is the Christian Science empire today?

Individual Cult Books (Specify title when ordering)   **$4.95**
Save $4.80! Buy All Four Books in the Series   **$15**

SALEM KIRBAN HEALTH BOOKS

Salem Kirban has spoken on Bible Prophecy in over 300 churches. Many times people, who were obviously ill, came to him asking for prayer. It was then Salem realized that he should write a few books on the Biblical approach to sound nutritional health!

HOW JUICES
RESTORE HEALTH NATURALLY
by Salem Kirban $4.95

Salem Kirban reveals how he found the Fountain of Youth **at age 50!** He tells his own experiences of how juices eliminated fatigue . . . gave him new vitality . . . a new lease on life. **Fourteen** different juice combinations illustrated in **FULL COLOR!**

HOW TO EAT YOUR WAY
BACK TO VIBRANT HEALTH
by Salem Kirban $3.95

Includes **147** different health restoring meals plus a special **3-Day Turn Around Diet!** Answers given to many questions people often ask about what foods to eat, how to have Reserve Energy, how to turn your marriage into a honeymoon!

HOW TO KEEP HEALTHY
AND HAPPY BY FASTING
by Salem Kirban $2.95

A best-selling book on Fasting that approaches the subject Biblically! Discover the secret of how fasting relieves tension, helps you sleep better, restores your energy level eliminating fatigue. Plus much more! Filled with photographs!

THE GETTING
BACK TO NATURE DIET
by Salem Kirban $3.95

Salem Kirban's best and most complete book on Health. Revealed at last! Nature's Secrets for keeping you well! **Only found in this book . . .** the most comprehensive Food Charts showing both **HIGH Stress** and **Low Stress** foods. Excellent!

SALEM KIRBAN, Inc., Kent Rd., Huntingdon Valley, Pa. 19006

Quantity	Description	Price	Total
_____	Charts On Revelation	$ 4.95	_____
_____	Countdown To Rapture	4.95	_____
_____	Guide To Survival	4.95	_____
_____	How To Be Sure Of Crowns In Heaven	4.95	_____
_____	How To Live Above Your Circumstances	4.95	_____
_____	Lebanon . . . A Harvest Of Love	3.95	_____
_____	Questions Frequently Asked Me On Prophecy	4.95	_____
_____	Revelation Visualized (September, 1980)	12.75	_____
_____	Satan's Angels Exposed	4.95	_____
_____	Satan's Music Exposed	4.95	_____
_____	666/1000	5.95	_____
_____	666 PICTORIAL FORMAT	2.95	_____
_____	The Rise Of Antichrist	4.95	_____
_____	Your Last Goodbye	4.95	_____
_____	Armstrong's Church Of God (Plain Truth)	4.95	_____
_____	Jehovah's Witnesses	4.95	_____
_____	Mormonism	4.95	_____
_____	Christian Science	4.95	_____
_____	How Juices Restore Health Naturally	4.95	_____
_____	How To Eat Your Way To Vibrant Health	3.95	_____
_____	How To Keep Healthy By Fasting	2.95	_____
_____	The Getting Back To Nature Diet	3.95	_____
_____	The Salem Kirban REFERENCE BIBLE	47.77	_____

Total for Books _____

Shipping & Handling _____

Total Enclosed $

(We do NOT invoice. Check must accompany order, please.)

☐ Check enclosed.
☐ Master Charge
☐ VISA

When using Credit Card, show number in space below.

When Using Master Charge
Also Give Interbank
No. (Just above your
name on card)

| Card Ex- pires | Month | Year |

POSTAGE & HANDLING Use this easy chart to figure postage, shipping and handling charges. Send correct amount and avoid delay.

TOTAL FOR BOOKS	Up to 5.00	5.01- 10.00	10.01- 20.00	20.01- 35.00	Over 35.00
DELIVERY CHARGE	1.50	2.00	2.50	2.95	NO CHARGE

FOR ADDITIONAL SAVINGS: Orders Over $35.00 Are Now Postage-Free!

SHIP TO_____

　　　Mr./Mrs./Miss　　　　(Please PRINT)

Address_____

City_____State_____ZIP_____

SALEM KIRBAN, Inc., Kent Rd., Huntingdon Valley, Pa. 19006

ORDER FORM　　　　　　　　　　SALEM KIRBAN Books

Quantity	Description	Price	Total
_____	Charts On Revelation	$ 4.95	_____
_____	Countdown To Rapture	4.95	_____
_____	Guide To Survival	4.95	_____
_____	How To Be Sure Of Crowns In Heaven	4.95	_____
_____	How To Live Above Your Circumstances	4.95	_____
_____	Lebanon . . . A Harvest Of Love	3.95	_____
_____	Questions Frequently Asked Me On Prophecy	4.95	_____
_____	Revelation Visualized (September, 1980)	12.75	_____
_____	Satan's Angels Exposed	4.95	_____
_____	Satan's Music Exposed	4.95	_____
_____	666/1000	5.95	_____
_____	666 PICTORIAL FORMAT	2.95	_____
_____	The Rise Of Antichrist	4.95	_____
_____	Your Last Goodbye	4.95	_____
_____	Armstrong's Church Of God (Plain Truth)	4.95	_____
_____	Jehovah's Witnesses	4.95	_____
_____	Mormonism	4.95	_____
_____	Christian Science	4.95	_____
_____	How Juices Restore Health Naturally	4.95	_____
_____	How To Eat Your Way To Vibrant Health	3.95	_____
_____	How To Keep Healthy By Fasting	2.95	_____
_____	The Getting Back To Nature Diet	3.95	_____
_____	The Salem Kirban REFERENCE BIBLE	47.77	_____

Total for Books _____

Shipping & Handling _____

Total Enclosed $

(We do NOT invoice. Check must accompany order, please.)

☐ Check enclosed.
☐ Master Charge
☐ VISA

When using Credit Card, show number in space below.

When Using Master Charge Also Give Interbank No. (Just above your name on card)

Card Expires	Month	Year

POSTAGE & HANDLING Use this easy chart to figure postage, shipping and handling charges. Send correct amount and avoid delay.

TOTAL FOR BOOKS	Up to 5.00	5.01-10.00	10.01-20.00	20.01-35.00	Over 35.00
DELIVERY CHARGE	1.50	2.00	2.50	2.95	NO CHARGE

FOR ADDITIONAL SAVINGS: Orders Over $35.00 Are Now Postage-Free!

SHIP TO_____
　　　Mr./Mrs./Miss　　　(Please PRINT)

Address_____

City_____State_____ZIP_____

SALEM KIRBAN, Inc., Kent Rd., Huntingdon Valley, Pa. 19006